# What People Are Saying About Joshua Mills and *Po*

STUDY GUIDE

# POWER
# PORTALS

STUDY GUIDE

# POWER PORTALS

AWAKEN YOUR CONNECTION TO
THE SPIRIT REALM

# JOSHUA MILLS

WHITAKER
HOUSE

*Publisher's Note*: This book is not intended to provide medical or psychological advice or to take the place of medical advice and treatment from your personal physician. Those who are having suicidal thoughts or who have been emotionally, physically, or sexually abused should seek help from a mental health professional or qualified counselor. Neither the publisher nor the author nor the author's ministry takes any responsibility for any possible consequences from any action taken by any person reading or following the information in this book. If readers are taking prescription medications, they should consult with their physicians and not take themselves off prescribed medicines without the proper supervision of a physician. Always consult your physician or other qualified health care professional before undertaking any change in your physical regimen, whether fasting, diet, medications, or exercise.

Unless otherwise indicated, all Scripture quotations are taken from the *King James Version Easy Read Bible*, kjver®, © 2001, 2007, 2010, 2015 by Whitaker House. Used by permission. All rights reserved. Scripture quotation marked (kjv) is taken from the King James Version of the Holy Bible. Scripture quotation marked (nkjv) is taken from the *New King James Version*, © 1979, 1980, 1982 by Thomas Nelson, Inc. Used by permission. All rights reserved. Scripture quotations marked (niv) are taken from the *Holy Bible, New International Version*®, niv®, © 1973, 1978, 1984, 2011 by Biblica, Inc.® Used by permission of Zondervan. All rights reserved worldwide. www.zondervan.com. The "NIV" and "New International Version" are trademarks registered in the United States Patent and Trademark Office by Biblica, Inc.® Scripture quotations marked (nlt) are taken from the *Holy Bible, New Living Translation*, © 1996, 2004, 2007 by Tyndale House Foundation. Used by permission of Tyndale House Publishers, Inc., Carol Stream, Illinois 60188. All rights reserved. Scripture quotations marked (amp) are taken from *The Amplified*® *Bible*, © 2015 by The Lockman Foundation, La Habra, CA. Used by permission. (www.Lockman.org). All rights reserved.

The forms Lord and God (in small caps) in Bible quotations represent the Hebrew name for God *Yahweh* (Jehovah), while *Lord* and *God* normally represent the name *Adonai*, in accordance with the Bible version used.

Boldface type in the Scripture quotations indicates the author's emphasis.

Definitions of Greek words marked (*Strong's*) are taken from *Strong's Exhaustive Concordance of the Bible*.

## Power Portals Study Guide
### Awaken Your Connection to the Spirit Realm

International Glory Ministries
P.O. Box 4037 • Palm Springs, CA 92263
JoshuaMills.com
info@joshuamills.com

ISBN: 978-1-64123-560-0
eBook ISBN: 978-1-64123-561-7
Printed in the United States of America
© 2020 by Joshua Mills

Whitaker House
1030 Hunt Valley Circle
New Kensington, PA 15068
www.whitakerhouse.com

1 2 3 4 5 6 7 8 9 10 11 12 ⨀ 29 28 27 26 25 24 23 22 21 20

# CONTENTS

# INTRODUCTION

I believe that the Holy Spirit has led you to the *Power Portals Study Guide* to be taught by the Lord. In these pages, you will receive supernatural training and equipping. This training and equipping will come alive within you not only as you read and embrace the revelation, but also as you activate it in your life.

It excites me to teach on the topic of divine power portals because, whenever I do, I see people being activated in their supernatural identities—awakening their connection to the Spirit realm. The same activation will happen for you!

This study guide works as a companion tool to my book *Power Portals,* so you will want to make sure you have both resources in your hands before you begin. The nine chapters in the book correspond to the nine lessons included here, but each lesson also contains some additional learning material with activations. Please take your time reading through the book and completing the assignments for each chapter. As you do, prepare to learn, to be challenged, and to embrace new spiritual realities as you engage with the revelation.

The message of *Power Portals* is both simple and complex. The message is simple because it is intended for every believer. Once you understand it, you can easily apply it to your daily life. If you follow the instructions, the results will be supernatural. The message is complex because there are many intricacies to the application of power portals. However, the *Power Portals* book and study guide are not intended to be a comprehensive review of all these intricacies. Rather, they are meant to be a launching pad to move you into the deeper things of God. Once you have launched out, you can trust the Spirit to continue to connect with your spirit and teach you further.

It is now my great joy and honor to welcome you to join me in discovering *Power Portals*. The Spirit is calling you. So, together, let's respond to His heavenly pull. Get ready to awaken your connection to the Spirit realm!

# HOW TO USE THIS STUDY GUIDE

The *Power Portals Study Guide* can be used for either individual or group study. For your convenience, an answer key is provided at the back of this study guide. Extra space is also included in the margins of each lesson for recording your thoughts, notes, and testimonies about how God is touching your life through divine power portals.

## TO FACILITATE PERSONAL STUDY

- Find a place that is comfortable for you and prepare this personal space by playing peaceful instrumental worship music. This will set the atmosphere for you to easily read the material, learn, and receive from the Spirit. Joshua Mills's albums *SpiritSpa* and *Experience His Glory* (available as CDs or digital music downloads) are excellent resources for this purpose.

- Always begin your time of study with a simple prayer, asking God to direct your thoughts and enable you to clearly understand the meaning of the words you read.

- There are a total of nine lessons in the *Power Portals Study Guide*. You can go through this curriculum at your own pace, but it is best to set a specific goal for finishing all of the studies to help you keep moving along to completion. You will find that the momentum will increase as you read through the lessons because each study builds upon the previous one.

- Remember to activate each lesson (apply it directly to your life as you allow the Spirit to minister to you) through direct engagement with the revelation that has been shared in the study.

- Most importantly…

Keep your eyes on Jesus…

Be anointed by His Spirit…

And experience *Power Portals*!

## TO FACILITATE A STUDY GROUP

- Prepare your meeting space with peaceful, instrumental worship music to set a spiritual atmosphere before the group begins to gather. Joshua Mills's albums *SpiritSpa* and *Experience His Glory* (available as CDs or digital music downloads) are excellent resources for this purpose.

- Always begin the meeting with a simple prayer, asking God to direct the conversation and bring divine understanding from the words that are read. As part of your prayer, you might speak this scriptural blessing over the group:

*I keep asking that the God of our Lord Jesus Christ, the glorious Father, may give you the Spirit of wisdom and revelation, so that you may know him better. I pray that the eyes of your heart may be enlightened in order that you may know the hope to which he has called you, the riches of his glorious inheritance in his holy people, and his incomparably great power for us who believe. That power is the same as the mighty strength he exerted when he raised Christ from the dead and seated him at his right hand in the heavenly realms.* (Ephesians 1:17–20 NIV)

- During the first meeting, ask each person to state their name and share their personal testimony in two minutes or less. Ask how everyone heard about the study group or why they are interested in learning about power portals. This will help the members of your group to become acquainted with one another and feel more at ease to participate.

- At all other meetings, ask questions such as the following to begin the conversation:
  - » "How did you like this week's chapter?"
  - » "Is there something from the book that you would especially like to discuss?"
  - » "Did anyone have a profound spiritual encounter (a dream, a miracle testimony, a personal revelation, an angelic experience, and so forth) through engaging with the concepts shared in the book?" (P.S.: Joshua would love to hear about them too! You can contact him at info@joshuamills.com.)

- You can encourage participants to read the recommended pages from the *Power Portals* books in advance, or you can ask people to take turns reading aloud in the corporate setting, depending upon your particular time restrictions and/or personal preferences.

- Always try to keep the conversation centered on the book content, but realize that you might not be able to cover all the points included in the study guide during the meeting. Don't feel pressured to complete all these points. Instead, see the study guide as a facilitator for discovering divine power portals.

- It is important to allow the Spirit to direct your conversation, so focus on the areas that He is emphasizing through the group discussion of the lesson content.

- Do a group activation so that everyone can directly engage with the revelation that has been shared within the specific lesson.

- To close the meeting, you can do one or more of the following:
  - » Use the last point in the study guide.
  - » Give a short closing prayer or ask another member of the group to do so.
  - » Corporately sing a worship song whose theme is related to the discussion.
  - » Thank everyone for coming.

- Sometimes, group facilitators choose to offer simple refreshments at the end of the meeting as a way to encourage fellowship and develop deeper community, giving people an opportunity to continue discussing the theme and sharing their lives. You may want to ask participants to take turns bringing the needed refreshments.

- You may want to consider scheduling a special "Glory Celebration," to be held after your last meeting, to commemorate your time together and make room to activate all the things you've learned. You could include a time of offering praise and worship, giving testimonies, and praying for one another, followed by more food and fellowship.

# PART I
## DISCOVERING POWER PORTALS

# WHAT IS A POWER PORTAL?

Before you begin this lesson, read chapter 1 of *Power Portals*.

*"Then as I looked, I saw a door standing open in heaven."*
—Revelation 4:1 (NLT)

## BECOMING ACQUAINTED WITH POWER PORTALS

- A portal is defined as "a doorway, gate, or other entrance, especially a large and imposing one."[1]

- "Portal" is just another way of saying "gateway."

- Today, God is giving us a heavenly vocabulary to articulate the divine, supernatural realms of glory we are experiencing.

- A power portal is a supernatural access point that enables us to transition from one place in our lives to another.

- When a power portal opens for us, it changes the atmosphere completely!

- If you are a believer in Jesus Christ, you are not a victim. Anything negative that happens in your life can be turned around by God, but you must give Him permission to do that.

## NEW DOORS ARE BEING OPENED

- All over the world, God is showing people visions of new doors being opened. For example, they are seeing the following:
    - » Golden gates

---

1. *OxfordDictionaries.com*, Oxford University Press, © 2020.

> » Large and imposing doors fashioned from ancient wood or burnished bronze
>
> » Openings of brilliant, swirling light

- These doors come with an invitation to step in.

## Q: HAVE YOU EVER SEEN A POWER PORTAL? IF SO, WHAT DID IT LOOK LIKE TO YOU?

- The apostle Paul said we would go *"from glory to glory"* (2 Corinthians 3:18), and that's exactly what is happening. God is opening doors of transition to take us from the limitations we have known into the fullness of all that He has promised.

- The spiritual realities that manifest in power portals have existed from eternity, and many believers over the centuries have experienced them.

- In our day, God's end-time purposes are moving toward their culmination. In fulfillment of His promises, God is preparing believers to regularly receive from power portals through the work of the Holy Spirit.

- God opened up the Red Sea to make a way of escape for the Israelites and to bring them through the wilderness to the promised land. Similarly, today, He is opening up power portals for His people to give us a way of escape and to secure our promised deliverance through unusual means.

## Q: DO YOU WANT TO ESTABLISH POWER PORTALS OVER YOUR HOME, YOUR FINANCIAL AFFAIRS, AND OTHER AREAS OF YOUR LIFE?

### PORTALS IN SCRIPTURE

- Paul had firsthand experience with power portals. The first encounter was on the road to Damascus, when he was still known as Saul. A blinding light came directly from heaven, shining upon him and knocking him to the ground. In this portal, God's voice spoke to Paul with clarity, giving him specific direction for his life.

READ: ACTS 9:3–9

- Through this encounter, God surely got Paul's attention! Whenever and wherever a portal opens, a great surge of spiritual power is released into the atmosphere and upon the people who are present there.

- When a portal opens over someone's life, there is an immediate spiritual shift.

- We find descriptions of portals as far back as the days of Jacob.

## READ: GENESIS 28:10–17

- This encounter caused Jacob to exclaim, *"This is the gate of heaven"* (Genesis 28:17). Jacob was declaring that a power portal had opened over his life in that moment.

### OTHER PORTALS MENTIONED IN THE SCRIPTURES

**Genesis 5:24 and Hebrews 11:5:** Enoch walked so closely with God that he did not die but was directly translated to heaven through a portal that was opened for him.

**Genesis 19:1:** Two angels appeared to Lot while he was sitting in the gateway (portal).

**Genesis 22:11–13:** When Abraham was about to sacrifice his son Isaac, the angel of the Lord stopped him and showed him God's supernatural provision, a ram caught by its horns in the thicket. Therefore, Abraham called that place on Mount Moriah (the Temple Mount) *"The Lord Will Provide"* (Genesis 22:14 NIV). The Scriptures further record, *"To this day it is said, 'On the mountain of the Lord it will be provided'"* (verse 14 NIV).

**Genesis 32:22–30:** Jacob had an encounter in which he wrestled with an angel. Afterward, Jacob called the place where this event occurred *Peniel*, which means "face of God."

**Leviticus 16:2 and Psalm 80:1:** The Most Holy Place, or the Holy of Holies, was a special location where the heavenly and the earthly intersected. It was an open portal of divine encounter in which God revealed His glorious presence and spoke to His people Israel.

**Joshua 3:11–17:** When God divided the waters of the Jordan River, and the children of Israel crossed to the other side, a portal was opened that has not been shut since. One of the reasons why Elijah later led Elisha to this specific location to strike the waters is that heavenly mantles are released in an open portal. (See 2 Kings 2:7–15.) Jesus was baptized in the Jordan, and this river continues to be a popular place for believers to be water baptized. People still have heavenly encounters in this portal.

**1 Kings 19:11–18:** On Mount Horeb, God spoke with Elijah, giving him revelation and direction.

**Proverbs 8:34:** This Scripture speaks about the blessing that comes to the person who listens and watches at the Lord's doorposts (portals).

**Ezekiel 1:1; 3:22–23; 8:1–2:** Ezekiel had several visions and encounters with the Lord as heavenly portals were opened for him. He described these occurrences as the hand of the Lord coming upon him.

**Daniel 12:3–4:** Daniel received revelation about personal portals being opened for those who were wise and willing to lead many to righteousness.

**John 1:51:** Jesus declared Himself to be a heavenly ladder, or portal, that would bring a vision of the open heavens to humanity.

**2 Corinthians 12:2–4 (NIV):** The apostle Paul was caught up into third-heaven encounters in which he heard *"inexpressible"* words that he was not given permission to speak about.

**Revelation 4:1; 11:12; 19:11:** While John the Revelator was exiled on the island of Patmos, he saw a door (portal) being opened, inviting him into heavenly prophetic encounters in which he received great insight about future events.

## WHAT HAPPENS IN A PORTAL?

1. A sudden, awesome realization comes. (See Genesis 28:17.)
2. An abundance of healing manifests. (See John 5:2–4.)
3. Spontaneous joy erupts. (See Psalm 16:11.)
4. Signs and wonders manifest. (See Acts 2:1–4.)
5. Angelic activity intensifies. (See Psalm 78:23–25.)
6. Spiritual dreams and visions increase. (See Ezekiel 1:1.)
7. Extravagant provision appears. (See Malachi 3:10–11.)

## FAITH ACTIVATES GOD'S POWER

- Faith creates a portal for God's supernatural provision to flow. Although God is sovereign and can independently act on our behalf, He desires that His people walk by faith. Through pure faith, God's chosen ones can activate His power in their lives.

## REVIEW QUESTIONS

(Page numbers correspond to the *Power Portals* book.)

1. Define the word *portal*. (p. 32)

    _____

    _____

    _____

2. God is opening _____ _____ _____ to take us from the limitations we have known into the fullness of all that He has promised. (p. 33)

3. What firsthand experience of power portals did Paul have? (p. 34)

    _____

    _____

    _____

4. Name several spiritual truths that Genesis 28 reveals from Jacob's experience of an open portal. (p. 36)

    _____

    _____

    _____

5. From the biblical examples in the *Power Portals* book and study guide, list three ways in which you can accurately discern that a power portal is being opened in your presence. (pp. 37–41)

    _____

    _____

    _____

6. God will open _____ _____ on earth to those who are willing to engage with _____. (p. 41)

7. Sometimes, power portals appear as visible, swirling lights. What is the spiritual meaning of the various colors in which they appear? (p. 31)

    _____

    _____

    _____

## ACTIVATIONS

1. **Spend Time with the Holy Spirit.** This is a personal activation. You can set a peaceful and worshipful atmosphere by dimming the lights (you might also choose to light a nice candle) and playing instrumental worship music, such as my *SpiritSpa* album or the instrumental tracks from my *Experience His Glory* album.

Once you settle into a comfortable position, either sitting in a soft chair or lying down, shut your eyes and begin reaching out to God through prayer. Be natural and have a conversation with your heavenly Father. You can confidently ask Him to show you new portals that He is opening for you because, throughout the Scriptures, you can see that it is God's will to open these gateways for you.

Relax and allow the Lord to paint pictures and bring other vivid images to you as you rest in Him. When you do this exercise, you may actually begin to hear the Spirit speak to your heart or impress an idea upon your spirit. Receive the message that God is lovingly bringing to you. Do not be in a rush. Enjoy spending time in the Lord's presence.

After being in the divine presence, you should feel refreshed and renewed. At this point, it would be helpful to either draw a picture, write down a description, or verbally dictate into a voice recorder the things you saw, heard, or felt while you were in the presence of the Lord. Meditate upon these things and ask yourself how you should respond to the Lord's beckoning.

At first, you might only see glimpses of images or discern short messages. Or, you might not see or discern anything at all. Don't be discouraged. That's okay. Make time in your schedule to repeat this exercise. The more you practice it, the more you will feel yourself opening up to the Spirit.

2. **Create a Portal!** You can use this activation as either a personal or group activity. Several years ago, while I was ministering at our Glory Institute at the Honolulu Convention Center in Hawaii, a man named John presented me with a beautiful gift. It was a small glass art piece that represented a heavenly power portal. He had been apprenticing in glassblowing and wanted to connect his knowledge of the glory with his love for the creative arts. It was beautiful. I keep that "portal" in my office, and whenever I look at it, I am reminded of the blessings that flow into my life when I experience God in His portals.

For this activation, I want you to connect your spirituality with the arts. Draw or paint a picture of what you think a power portal might look like. There is no right or wrong way to do this. Some may visualize it as a large and imposing door, while others may see it as a brilliant opening of light or a swirling mass of colors. Be creative and allow the flow of the Holy Spirit to lead you. If you struggle with creativity, ask the Spirit to help you express yourself in this way.

If you really don't enjoy painting or drawing, try writing a description of a portal. Your word creation should remind you of the Spirit's blessings and help you to focus on Jesus Christ and His goodness!

# FINDING YOUR WAY

Before you begin this lesson, read chapter 2 of *Power Portals*.

*"Ask and it will be given to you; seek and you will find; knock and the door will be opened to you."*
—Matthew 7:7 (NIV)

## YOU SHALL KNOW THE TRUTH

- Many people rely entirely on their own intellect and perceptions, proud to live according to what they call their "own truth." A big problem with this approach is that their perceived truth is usually variable.

- *"They perish because they refused to love the truth and so be saved"* (2 Thessalonians 2:10 NIV).

## Q: WHAT DOES THIS SCRIPTURE MEAN TO YOU? WHAT IS THE TRUTH?

## ASK, SEEK, KNOCK

- The person who relies on their own wisdom and understanding will never come to a knowledge of eternal truth. However, those who earnestly search for the true God will find the truth they are looking for.

- *"But when he, the Spirit of truth, comes, he will guide you into all the truth. He will not speak on his own; he will speak only what he hears, and he will tell you what is yet to come"* (John 16:13 NIV).

### A LIVING PORTAL

- Jesus is the door to true life. His Spirit leads us into truth. (See John 16:13.)

- *"Verily, verily, I say to you, **I am the door of the sheep**. All that ever came before Me are thieves and robbers: but the sheep did not hear them. **I am the door**: by Me if any man enter in, he shall be saved, and shall go in and out, and find pasture. The thief comes not, but for to steal, and to kill, and to destroy: I am come that they might have life, and that they might have it more abundantly"* (John 10:7–10).

- Jesus was telling us that there is one appropriate way into the realm of the supernatural, or the realm of God's glory. It is the only legal entryway into this realm. We must go through the gate, or the power portal, that He has provided.

- *"I am the way, the truth, and the life: no man comes to the Father, but by Me"* (John 14:6).

## Q: HAVE YOU EVER EXPERIENCED JESUS AS A LIVING DOORWAY? WHAT NEW THINGS OR NEW PLACES HAS HE INTRODUCED YOU TO IN THE SPIRITUAL REALM?

### MANY ENTRANCES, BUT ONLY ONE DOOR

- People who follow New Age teachings attempt to gain access into the supernatural realm by their own merits, but that is illegal, spiritually speaking. People who engage in various occult practices also try to connect with the supernatural, but their teachings and methods are dark and prohibited by God and, therefore, illegal as well.

## Q: WHAT HAPPENS IF YOU DO SOMETHING ILLEGAL IN THE NATURAL REALM?

- Jesus said that there is only one way into the divine supernatural, and that is through the portal of God's glory.

### JESUS, OUR PORTAL INTO HEAVENLY GLORY

- Jesus is our portal into heavenly glory. He is the way.

- Jesus is our means of access to God.

- Jesus referred to Himself as *"the narrow gate."* (See Matthew 7:13–14.)

- To give up our life for Jesus's sake is the way of love. Will you allow Him entrance into your heart? This is the way the portal opens.

## THE SEVENFOLD PORTAL

- Jesus is our portal into truth and life. In fact, according to the Scriptures, in Christ, you can find at least seven specific portals of access:

  1. He is the only portal to the life of God. (See Matthew 7:14.)

  2. He is the portal of escape. (See 1 Corinthians 10:13.)

  3. He is the portal into the Holiest. (See Hebrews 9:11–12.)

  4. He is the portal into *"a new and living way."* (See Hebrews 10:20.)

  5. He is the portal of truth. (See 2 Peter 2:2.)

  6. He is the portal into the *"right way."* (See 2 Peter 2:15.)

  7. He is the portal of righteousness. (See 2 Peter 2:21.)

- When we are in Christ, we have the ability to bypass the second-heaven realm of demonic warfare and torment.

- We enter the third heaven through the blood of Jesus Christ and the finished work that He provided for us on the cross of Calvary.

## THE LOWER YOU GO, THE HIGHER YOU RISE

- When we humble ourselves in worship before God's majesty, we discover the greatest heights of His heavenly glory.

- Our sole responsibility is to live our lives in a way that will honor and worship Jesus in and through everything we do.

- When you realize that Jesus is the door, He becomes your primary focus.

## Q: WHAT DOES IT MEAN TO LOWER YOURSELF TO WHOLEHEARTEDLY PURSUE JESUS?

## THE PORTALS OF JESUS'S NAME

- Jesus asked His disciples, *"Who do you say I am?"* (Matthew 16:15 NIV).

- There are approximately two hundred names for God the Son in the Bible.

- For believers, every single one of Jesus's names becomes a portal that we are invited to explore.

Advocate (1 John 2:1)

Alpha and Omega (Revelation 1:8, 11)

The Amen (Revelation 3:14)

The Ancient of Days (Daniel 7:22)

The Anointed (Luke 4:18)

The Apostle (Hebrews 3:1)

The Author and Finisher of Our Faith
(Hebrews 12:2)

The Beginning and the End
(Revelation 22:13)

The Beloved (Ephesians 1:6)

Bishop of Our Souls (1 Peter 2:25)

Branch of Righteousness (Jeremiah 33:15)

Bread of Life (John 6:35)

Bridegroom (Matthew 9:15)

Bright and Morning Star (Revelation 22:16)

Captain of Our Salvation (Hebrews 2:10)

Chief Cornerstone (Ephesians 2:20)

Chosen One (Luke 23:35)

Christ (Matthew 16:16)

Consolation of Israel (Luke 2:25)

Covert from the Tempest (Isaiah 32:2)

Creator (Colossians 1:16)

Dayspring (Luke 1:78)

Daystar (2 Peter 1:19)

Deliverer (Romans 11:26)

The Desire of All Nations (Haggai 2:7)

The Door (John 10:7, 9)

Emmanuel (Matthew 1:23)

Eternal Life (John 10:27–28)

Express Image of God (Hebrews 1:3)

Faithful Witness (Revelation 1:5)

The First and the Last (Revelation 2:8)

Firstborn of the Dead (Revelation 1:5)

The Firstfruits (1 Corinthians 15:23)

Forerunner (Hebrews 6:20)

Friend of Sinners (Matthew 11:19)

God's Elect (Isaiah 42:1)

Good Shepherd (John 10:11)

Governor (Matthew 2:6)

Great High Priest (Hebrews 4:14)

Great Shepherd of the Sheep
(Hebrews 13:20)

God's Messiah (Luke 23:35)

Habitation (Psalm 91:9)

Head of the Church (Colossians 1:18)

Healer (Exodus 15:26)

Heir of All Things (Hebrews 1:2)

Hidden Manna (Revelation 2:17)

Hiding Place (Psalm 32:7)

Highway of Holiness (Isaiah 35:8)

Holy Child (Acts 4:30)

Holy One (Mark 1:24)

Hope of Israel (Acts 28:20)

Intercessor (Romans 8:34)

Judge of All (Acts 10:42)

King (Matthew 21:5)

King of Kings (1 Timothy 6:15)

The Lamb (Revelation 17:14)

The Lamb of God (John 1:29)

The Last/Second Adam
(1 Corinthians 15:45)

Leader (Isaiah 55:4)

The Life (John 11:25)

Light of the World (John 8:12)

Lily of the Valley (Song of Solomon 2:1)

Lion of the Tribe of Judah (Revelation 5:5)

Living Bread (John 6:51)

Lord (Romans 1:3)

Lord of Hosts (Jeremiah 32:18)

Lord of Lords (Revelation 17:14)

The Lord Our Righteousness
   (Jeremiah 23:6)

Man (Acts 17:31)

Man of War (Isaiah 42:13)

Master (Matthew 8:19)

Mediator (1 Timothy 2:5)

Messiah (Daniel 9:25)

Mighty God (Isaiah 9:6)

Mighty One of Israel (Isaiah 1:24)

Mighty One of Jacob (Isaiah 60:16)

Minister (Hebrews 8:2)

My Shepherd (Psalm 23:1)

Nazarene (Matthew 2:23)

Offering (Ephesians 5:2)

Offspring of David (Revelation 22:16)

Only Begotten (John 1:14)

Our Hope (1 Timothy 1:1)

Our Passover (1 Corinthians 5:7)

Physician (Luke 4:23)

Potentate (1 Timothy 6:15)

Power of God (1 Corinthians 1:24)

Prince of Life (Acts 3:15)

Prince of Peace (Isaiah 9:6)

Prophet (Acts 3:22)

Propitiation (1 John 2:2)

Radiance of God's Glory (Hebrews 1:3)

Ransom (1 Timothy 2:6)

Redeemer (Isaiah 59:20)

Refiner and Purifier (Malachi 3:3)

The Resurrection (John 11:25)

Righteousness (1 Corinthians 1:30)

Rock (1 Corinthians 10:4)

Rod and Branch (Isaiah 11:1)

Root of David (Revelation 22:16)

Rose of Sharon (Song 2:1)

Ruler in Israel (Micah 5:2)

Sacrifice (Ephesians 5:2)

Sanctification (1 Corinthians 1:30)

Savior (Acts 5:31)

Scepter out of Israel (Numbers 24:17)

Seed of Abraham (Galatians 3:29)

Seed of David (2 Timothy 2:8)

Servant of God (Isaiah 42:1)

Shadow of a Great Rock (Isaiah 32:2)

Shepherd of Israel (Psalm 80:1)

Shepherd of Our Souls (1 Peter 2:25)

Shiloh (Genesis 49:10)

The Son of God (Matthew 4:3)

The Son of Man (Matthew 8:20)

The Son of the Highest (Luke 1:32)

The Son of the Living God (Matthew 16:16)

Sower of Good Seed (Matthew 13:3-8)

Star out of Jacob (Numbers 24:17)

The Stone of Israel (Genesis 49:24)

Sun of Righteousness (Malachi 4:2)

Sure Foundation (Isaiah 28:16)

Teacher from God (John 3:2)

Testator (Hebrews 9:16)

The True God (1 John 5:20)

The True Vine (John 15:1)

The Truth (John 14:6)

Unspeakable Gift of God
   (2 Corinthians 9:15)

The Way (John 14:6)

The Wisdom of God (1 Corinthians 1:24)

Wonderful Counselor (Isaiah 9:6)

The Word (John 1:1)

The Word of God (Revelation 19:13)

Worthy (Revelation 5:12)

**FAITH CONNECTS TO ANOINTING**

- Faith in Jesus unlocks the door for us to experience the power of the Holy Spirit in our lives in a tangible way.

- We are connected to heaven's power source through the infilling of the Spirit, which brings with it a supernatural ability to do the works of God. (See Acts 1:8.)

- As we are filled, we are positioned to release greater power everywhere we go.

- In order to receive the Holy Spirit's infilling, all you need to do is ask Him to come and fill you, to live inside you with His power.

READ: LUKE 11:9–13

## REVIEW QUESTIONS

(Page numbers correspond to the *Power Portals* book.)

1.  What was Jesus speaking about in Matthew 7:7? (p. 45)

    _____

    _____

    _____

2.  Jesus said that there is only one way into the divine supernatural, and that is through the

    _____ ____ _____ _____. (p. 47)

3.  Jesus is the _____, the power portal for the sheep (God's sons and daughters). He Himself is

    the only _____, the only legal means of entry into the divine supernatural. (p. 48)

4.  Describe your experience of accepting Jesus as personal Lord and Savior of your life:

    _____

    _____

    _____

    _____

    _____

5.  Write out what Jesus said in John 14:6: (p. 50)

    _____

    _____

    _____

6.  List at least three of the seven specific ways in which Jesus is the ultimate power portal, providing
    us access to the Spirit realm: (pp. 50–51)

    _____

    _____

    _____

7.  The infilling of the Spirit releases us into the flow of heaven, opening up power portals

    _____ us, _____ us and, most importantly, _____ us. (p. 58)

## ACTIVATIONS

1. **Pray to Receive the Infilling.** As a personal activation, go to pages 59–60 in *Power Portals*. Follow the three keys to receiving the Spirit's infilling, praying the prayer that is provided. If you have already received the baptism in the Holy Spirit, I want to remind you that you can and should always receive fresh infillings of the Spirit. Acts 13:52 says, *"And the disciples were continually filled [throughout their hearts and souls] with joy and with the Holy Spirit"* (AMP).

2. **Become a Catalyst for Breakthrough.** As a group activation, the leader can invite members to discuss ways in which they have personally encountered one of the sevenfold portals of access to the Spirit realm that Jesus provides. After a member shares a short testimony, they can ask others in the room if they are in need of experiencing Christ in the same way. The individual's testimony can become a catalyst for others to receive their supernatural breakthroughs as you pray about their needs. Continue in this way as the Spirit leads and as time permits. The leader might also ask each participant to commit to journaling the ways they notice Christ as a sevenfold portal in the week ahead, with participants sharing their testimonies at the next gathering.

3. **Discover the Portals of Jesus's Name.** This activation is for either personal or group application. After saying a short prayer thanking Jesus for the access you find in Him, take a moment to consider the current situations and needs you are facing in your life. We know that for every need, Christ *is* the answer. Next, review the various names of Jesus listed in this lesson and find one that seems to resonate with you in your current season. Once you find that specific name, write it down and commit to using it in prayer, worship, and personal reflection. In this way, you will begin to discover the portal of Jesus's name. Expect miracles, victories, and special blessings to follow. In a group setting, the members might worship together using the names they have selected. Or, each participant might pray a sentence using their selected name as you go around the room opening a corporate portal for encounter.

# RECOGNIZING CHRIST IN YOU

Before you begin this lesson, read chapter 3 of *Power Portals*.

*"This is the secret: Christ lives in you. This gives you assurance of sharing his glory."*
—Colossians 1:27 (NLT)

## THE GREATEST DISCOVERIES

- In a prophetic word, the Lord said, "The greatest discoveries in the days ahead will be in outer space and inner space."

- "Outer space" refers to the three heavens and their interactions with one another.

- "Inner space" refers to the "space" within us. God has deposited heavenly potential inside each and every person, potential we have yet to explore.

- Encountering these depths can be our greatest discovery!

## Q: WHAT ARE THE IMPLICATIONS OF THESE TRUTHS FOR YOUR OWN LIFE?

## NEW-CREATION REALITIES

- *"It doesn't matter whether we have been circumcised or not. What counts is whether we have been transformed into a new creation"* (Galatians 6:15 NLT).

- What really matters is God's work in us. The finished work of Christ on Calvary has given us the ability to become new creations. Now, we must learn how to live according to the new-creation reality within us.

- *"Therefore if anyone is in Christ [that is, grafted in, joined to Him by faith in Him as Savior], he is a new creature [reborn and renewed by the Holy Spirit]; the old things [the previous moral and spiritual condition] have passed away. Behold, new things have come [because spiritual awakening brings new life]"* (2 Corinthians 5:17 AMP).

- The term *"new creation* or *"new creature"* signifies that you are a species of being that has never existed before.

- Scientists tell us that a caterpillar's body actually melts inside its chrysalis, liquefying and becoming a gooey ooze. Old things are in the process of passing away. The caterpillar becomes an entirely new entity—a butterfly. For example:

  » It goes into the cocoon with a chewing mouth but comes out with a sucking mouth.

  » The body of a caterpillar has three main parts—head, thorax, and abdomen—with thirteen segments within its thorax and abdomen. The body of a butterfly also has three main parts—head, thorax (with wings), and abdomen—but without the segments found in a caterpillar.

  » A caterpillar has twelve eyes, but it is still limited by a primitive sense of light and dark. A butterfly has two compound eyes with thousands of lenses and can see in full, living color.

## Q: HOW DO YOU SEE THIS EXAMPLE IN COMPARISON TO A PERSON WHO RECEIVES NEW LIFE THROUGH CHRIST?

### SPIRIT EYES

- Ezekiel and John the Revelator both saw heavenly creatures covered with eyes.

## READ: EZEKIEL 10:12; REVELATION 4:6, 8

- The eyes of these heavenly creatures are open to the ever-expanding revelation of the Lord God Almighty and His greatness.

- God wants to give us eyes in the Spirit, eyes that can truly see, so that we might view Him as He is.

- We need to see ourselves in the same way in which God sees us. God looks at us as completely cleansed through the blood of Jesus.

- Many blessings are available to you in the glory realm, but you first have to open your spiritual eyes to see them.

Q: WHAT TYPES OF THINGS HAVE YOU SEEN IN THE SPIRITUAL REALM? HOW HAS THIS REVELATION IMPACTED YOUR LIFE AS A BELIEVER?

## DISCOVERING YOUR GOD-POTENTIAL

- There is so much potential inside you! God Himself put it there.

- God desires to open new power portals for you, but you have to be receptive to the idea of greater and wider spiritual realms.

- The Bible records that a number of God's followers were taken into supernatural experiences where they were transported through a power portal from one place to another. For example:

  » Enoch faithfully walked with God, and then, one day, he was suddenly taken to heaven by the Lord without experiencing death. (See Genesis 5:24.)

  » The prophet Elijah was commonly "taken up" in power portal encounters. (See, for example, 1 Kings 18:11–12.)

  » The prophet Ezekiel was lifted up and carried away by the Spirit, who transported him fifteen hundred miles. By supernatural means, Ezekiel physically traveled this great distance. (See Ezekiel 3:12–15.)

  » Jesus and His disciples, while still in their boat, were instantly transported from the middle of the lake to the shore. (See John 6:16–20.)

  » The disciple Philip was caught up by the Spirit and carried approximately twenty miles up the coast. (See Acts 8:39–40.)

- Don't be surprised if a power portal suddenly opens. God has a way of supernaturally moving His people for His purposes!

Q: WHEN POWER PORTALS OPEN UP, HOW DO THEY MANIFEST? (THERE IS AN EXAMPLE ON PAGE 72 IN THE *POWER PORTALS* BOOK.)

- Power portals can open up around us as spheres of protection.

## READ: ISAIAH 60:1–3

- No matter where you are in life or what you are currently going through, there are realms of glory available for you to access.

- There are things coming on the earth in the days ahead that will look like terrible tragedies, immense devastation, but, just as we read in Isaiah 60, as the darkness increases, the glory of God will shine ever brighter.

- There are supernatural provisions for us in power portals.

## READ: DANIEL 3

Q: WHAT HAPPENED TO SHADRACH, MESHACH, AND ABEDNEGO AFTER THEY WERE THROWN INTO A FURNACE BY KING NEBUCHADNEZZAR? HOW DOES THIS INCIDENT RELATE TO POWER PORTALS AND GOD'S PROVISION FOR YOU?

### THE PORTAL OF GOD'S WORD

- We can receive God in an undiluted way through His Word.

- As we believe and speak the promises in the Bible, the miraculous results we see are physical manifestations of spiritual realities.

- God's Word offers us opportunities to discover countless portals. Whatever you need can be found in the Word.

### *WHO I AM ACCORDING TO GOD'S WORD*

**I am** the salt of the earth. (Matthew 5:13)

**I am** the light of the world. (Matthew 5:14)

**I am** a supernatural being who demonstrates God's supernatural power. (Mark 16:17)

**I am** a miracle worker. (Mark 16:20)

**I am** a child of God. (John 1:12)

**I am** part of the True Vine. (John 15:1, 5)

**I am** Christ's friend. (John 15:15)

**I am** chosen and appointed by Christ to bear His fruit. (John 15:16)

**I am** a servant/slave of righteousness. (Romans 6:18)

**I am** servant/slave of God. (Romans 6:22)

**I am** a son or daughter of God. (Romans 8:14–15; Galatians 3:26; 4:6)

**I am** an heir of God and a joint-heir with Christ. (Romans 8:17; Galatians 4:6–7)

**I am** God's temple. His Spirit and His life dwell in me. (1 Corinthians 3:16; 6:19)

**I am** united to the Lord and am one spirit with Him. (1 Corinthians 6:17)

**I am** a member of Christ's body. (1 Corinthians 12:27; Ephesians 5:30)

**I am** a new creation. (2 Corinthians 5:17)

**I am** reconciled to God and am a minister of peace and reconciliation. (2 Corinthians 5:18–19)

**I am** a child of God and one in Christ with other believers. (Galatians 3:26, 28)

**I am** a saint. (1 Corinthians 1:2; Ephesians 1:1; Philippians 1:1; Colossians 1:2)

**I am** God's workmanship. (Ephesians 2:10)

**I am** strong in the Lord and in the power of His might. (Ephesians 6:10)

**I am** justified by faith, completely forgiven and made righteous. (Romans 5:1)

**I am** dead to sin. (Romans 6:1–7)

**I am** free forever from condemnation. (Romans 8:1)

**I am** anointed by the Holy Spirit. (2 Corinthians 1:21; Ephesians 1:13–14)

**I am** righteous with Jesus's righteousness. (2 Corinthians 5:21)

**I am** blessed with every spiritual blessing. (Ephesians 1:3)

**I am** without blame before God. (Ephesians 1:4)

**I am** adopted as God's child. (Ephesians 1:5)

**I am** redeemed and forgiven. (Colossians 1:14; 2:13)

**I am** a recipient of God's lavish grace. (Ephesians 1:7)

**I am** connected with God through His Spirit. (Ephesians 2:18)

**I am** confident to approach God's throne. (Ephesians 3:12; Hebrews 4:16)

**I am** rescued from all harm. (Colossians 1:13)

**I am** debt-free. (Colossians 2:14)

**I am** firmly rooted in Christ and am now being built up in Him. (Colossians 2:7)

**I am** complete in Christ. (Colossians 2:10)

**I am** operating in a spirit of power, love, and a sound mind. (2 Timothy 1:7)

**I am** sanctified, and Jesus is not ashamed to call me brother or sister. (Hebrews 2:11)

**I am** healed. (1 Peter 2:24)

**I am** a partaker of God's divine nature. (2 Peter 1:4)

**I am** a fellow citizen with the rest of God's family. (Ephesians 2:19)

**I am** a prisoner of Christ. (Ephesians 3:1; 4:1)

**I am** righteous and holy. (Ephesians 4:24)

**I am** a citizen of heaven. (Philippians 3:20)

**I am** seated in heavenly places in Christ. (Ephesians 2:6)

**I am** hidden with Christ in God. (Colossians 3:3)

**I am** an expression of the life of Christ. (Colossians 3:4)

**I am** chosen of God, holy, and dearly loved. (Colossians 3:12; 1 Thessalonians 1:4)

**I am** a child of light. (1 Thessalonians 5:5)

**I am** a holy partaker of the heavenly calling. (Hebrews 3:1)

**I am** a partaker of Christ; I share in His life. (Hebrews 3:14)

**I am** a living stone. (1 Peter 2:5)

**I am** God's own possession. (1 Peter 2:9–10)

**I am** a stranger and pilgrim in this world. (1 Peter 2:11)

**I am** an enemy of the devil. (1 Peter 5:8)

**I am** a child of God and will resemble Christ when He returns. (1 John 3:1–2)

**I am** born of God, and the enemy cannot touch me. (1 John 5:18)

**I am** what I am by the grace of God. (1 Corinthians 15:10)

## UNTAPPED POTENTIAL

- Jesus Christ is the hope of glory, and if He is living inside you, there is potential there that you have not yet tapped into. Ask the Holy Spirit to reveal this potential to you. When He does, release it and do what He leads you to do.

- Draw close to God and allow the Holy Spirit to direct you in the ways He has planned for you, which are *"exceeding abundantly above all that* [you] *ask or think"* (Ephesians 3:20).

- No matter what you face in life, Jesus is always an open door. He has said that old things have passed away, and all things have become brand-new. Believe it and act on it!

## REVIEW QUESTIONS

(Page numbers correspond to the *Power Portals* book.)

1. There are depths of the Spirit, even _____ and _____, within us. Encountering these depths can be our greatest discovery! (p. 63)

2. We must learn how to live according to the _____-_____ reality within us. (p. 64)

3. Why did the heavenly creatures that John saw cry, *"Holy, holy, holy"*? (p. 66)

   _____

   _____

   _____

   _____

   _____

4. God desires to open new power portals for you, but you have to be receptive to the idea of _____ and _____ spiritual realms. (p. 71)

5. Describe the testimony that impacted you the most while reading this chapter.

   _____

   _____

   _____

   _____

   _____

6. Every testimony in the sacred Scriptures offers you an opportunity to enter into something bigger than _____. (pp. 74–75)

7. God has given you of His _____. He has put a _____ and _____ inside you, and you have _____ _____, ability, and creative power to find solutions to your everyday problems.

## ACTIVATIONS

1. **Discover the Portal of God's Word.** Use this activation as either a personal or group activity. Below, you will find that I've adapted a biblical account to give you the opportunity to find yourself and others in it. You will use this story to open a portal of healing for someone in need. I want you to see yourself and your loved ones in God's Word, recognizing that Jesus's miracles can become very personal to you. Ask the Lord for the name of someone whom you can apply to this account. Once you have that name, take some time to fill in the blanks, and then reread the story with conviction.

*When Jesus returned to* _____ *(your city),* _____ *(your name) came and pleaded with him, "Lord, my* _____ *(friend, child, spouse, parent) lies in bed,* _____ *(name of sickness) and in terrible pain."*

*Jesus said, "I will come and heal [them]."*

*But* _____ *(your name) said, "Lord, I am not worthy to have you come.... Just say the word from where you are, and* _____ *(name of the sick person) will be healed."...*

*When Jesus heard this, he was amazed. Turning to those who were following him, he said, "I tell you the truth, I haven't seen faith like this in all* _____ *(your country)!"...*

*Then Jesus said to* _____ *(your name), "Go back.... Because you believed, it has happened."* *And* _____ *(name of sick person) was healed that same hour.*    (Matthew 8:5–8, 10, 13 NLT)

This is one of the ways you can open up the portal of God's Word. When you see yourself and your loved ones within the Word, a supernatural door opens for you.

After completing this exercise, search through the Scriptures to find a story you feel spiritually connected to. For example, if you're in need of a miracle, you might want to find another story about Jesus working miracles. If you're dealing with lack, you might want to find a story about God's extravagant provision. As you read the story out loud (whether by yourself or in a group), see yourself in the position of the person receiving the miracle. This will help you to make a connection between the words on the page and the living Word of God manifesting for you today. Feel free to read this story as many times as you need to. Each time, focus on God's loving concern for you. As you do this, a power portal will begin to open for you to receive the benefit of the Word.

2. **Decree "I Am" Statements.** As a personal or group activation, use the "Who I Am According to God's Word" list in this lesson. Write out three "I am" statements that you will decree throughout this week, along with their corresponding Scriptures. Speaking these "I am" declarations out loud will give you greater confidence in recognizing Christ in you, and something will supernaturally shift within you.

# PART II
# ALIGNING WITH POWER PORTALS

LESSON 4

# THE HEAVENS ARE OPEN

Before you begin this lesson, read chapter 4 of *Power Portals*.

*"The heavens were opened, and I saw visions of God."*
—Ezekiel 1:1

## CAUGHT UP IN A HEAVENLY VISION

- *"Blessed are the pure in heart: for they shall see God"* (Matthew 5:8).

- During a supernatural encounter, the Lord said to me, "My abundance comes as My Spirit and truth are revealed and accepted."

## Q: WHAT DO THESE WORDS MEAN TO YOU? HOW DO THEY SPEAK INTO YOUR LIFE RIGHT NOW?

- When power portals open, they extend from the heavens to the earth. We can be drawn up into a portal to see a vision, but then we are returned to the earth so that the portal can be released through us as we take new steps of faith.

## AN OPEN HEAVEN OVER IQALUIT

- The Bible is clear that power portals can open over our personal lives.

- Power portals can also open in greater magnitude over a region that we "occupy" with spiritual authority.

# Q: HAVE YOU SEEN A POWER PORTAL OPEN OVER A REGION? IF SO, WHERE, AND WHAT WERE THE RESULTS?

- *"If My people, which are called by My name, shall humble themselves, and pray, and seek My face, and turn from their wicked ways: then will I hear from heaven, and will forgive their sin, and will heal their land"* (2 Chronicles 7:14).
- There is a very real connection between personal prayer and repentance and the healing of our lands.

## OPEN HEAVENS AROUND THE WORLD

- Each portal has the ability to open additional portals.

# Q: WHAT DOES THIS STATEMENT MEAN? HOW WOULD SUCH AN OCCURRENCE UNFOLD? (THERE IS AN EXAMPLE ON PAGES 85–86 IN THE *POWER PORTALS* BOOK.)

- One revival can activate another, each containing its own distinct anointing and emphasis.
- Each power portal has a divine purpose. We can see this element clearly in the biblical example of Israel.

## AN OPEN HEAVEN OVER ISRAEL

- Jerusalem is positioned as the center of the world.
- *"This is what the Sovereign LORD says: This is Jerusalem, which I have set in the center of the nations, with countries all around her"* (Ezekiel 5:5 NIV).
- Spiritually speaking, Jerusalem is one of the most powerfully charged places on earth.
- The largest portal on earth is located over the entire nation of Israel.
- People of faith create spiritual vortexes in various places.
- Through scientific study, we've learned that all matter has memory. This means that, in some way, the land, stones, and relics of the biblical world are all still resonating with a consciousness of the past.
- Site after site offers a chance for today's believers to connect their living faith with the faith of the ancients.

# Q: HAVE YOU BEEN TO ISRAEL, AND IF SO, WERE YOU AWARE OF AN OPEN PORTAL AT ANY OF THE HOLY SITES THAT YOU VISITED?

### OPEN-HEAVEN VISIONS THROUGHOUT SCRIPTURE
(All Scriptures in this section are from *The Amplified Bible*.)

*So [Jacob] was afraid and said, "How fearful and awesome is this place! This is none other than the house of God, and this is the gateway to heaven."* (Genesis 28:17)

*Micaiah said, "Therefore, hear the word of the LORD. I saw the LORD sitting on His throne, and all the host (army) of heaven standing by Him on His right hand and on His left."* (1 Kings 22:19)

*Then Elisha prayed and said, "LORD, please, open his eyes that he may see." And the LORD opened the servant's eyes and he saw; and behold, the mountain was full of horses and chariots of fire surrounding Elisha.* (2 Kings 6:17)

*Now it came about [when I was] in my thirtieth year [of life], on the fifth day of the fourth month, while I was among the exiles beside the River Chebar [in Babylonia], the heavens were opened and I saw visions of God.* (Ezekiel 1:1)

*In the visions of God He brought me to the land of Israel and set me down on a very high mountain, on the south side of which there was what seemed to be a structure of a city.* (Ezekiel 40:2)

*Then the secret was revealed to Daniel in a vision of the night, and Daniel blessed the God of heaven.* (Daniel 2:19)

*I kept looking in the night visions, and behold, on the clouds of heaven one like a Son of Man was coming, and He came up to the Ancient of Days and was presented before Him.* (Daniel 7:13)

*Then I looked up, and there were two women coming out with the wind in their wings; and they had wings like the wings of a stork, and they lifted up the ephah between the earth and the heavens.* (Zechariah 5:9)

*In those days Jesus came from Nazareth of Galilee and was baptized by John in the Jordan. Immediately coming up out of the water, he (John) saw the heavens torn open, and the Spirit like a dove descending on Him (Jesus); and a voice came out of heaven saying: "You are My beloved Son, in You I am well-pleased and delighted!"* (Mark 1:9–11)

*But [Stephen], being full of the Holy Spirit and led by Him, gazed into heaven and saw the glory [the great splendor and majesty] of God, and Jesus standing at the right hand of God; and he said, "Look! I see the heavens opened up [in welcome] and the Son of Man standing at the right hand of God!"* (Acts 7:55–56)

*And [Peter] saw the sky opened up, and an object like a great sheet descending, lowered by its four corners to the earth.* (Acts 10:11)

*So, King Agrippa, I [Paul] was not disobedient to the heavenly vision.* (Acts 26:19)

*I know a man in Christ who fourteen years ago—whether in the body I do not know, or out of the body I do not know, [only] God knows—such a man was caught up to the third heaven.* (2 Corinthians 12:2)

*They serve as a pattern and foreshadowing of [what has its true existence and reality in] the heavenly things (sanctuary). For when Moses was about to erect the tabernacle, he was warned by God, saying, "See that you make it all [exactly] according to the pattern which was shown to you on the mountain."* (Hebrews 8:5)

*After this I looked, and behold, a door standing open in heaven! And the first voice which I had heard, like the sound of a [war] trumpet speaking with me, said, "Come up here, and I will show you what must take place after these things."* (Revelation 4:1)

*And I saw heaven opened, and behold, a white horse, and He who was riding it is called Faithful and True (trustworthy, loyal, incorruptible, steady), and in righteousness He judges and wages war [on the rebellious nations].* (Revelation 19:11)

*And I saw the holy city, new Jerusalem, coming down out of heaven from God, arrayed like a bride adorned for her husband.* (Revelation 21:2)

## THE SWIRLINGS OF GOD

- When you set your mind upon Jesus, especially in worship, it's quite amazing the places where you can go and the way the Spirit begins to move within you.

- We step into new territories of worship as we allow the Spirit to lead us in new songs, new sounds, and new rhythms.

- If we give ourselves permission to yield and sing the new, spontaneous songs of the Lord, it will bring us into a new vision of His majesty. This is how we inwardly transcend the atmospheric confinements of the earth and begin moving higher in the Spirit.

- Heaven responds by surrounding us with divine "swirlings."

Q: IN THIS CONTEXT, WHAT DOES THE WORD *SWIRLINGS* MEAN TO YOU? WHAT DOES A SWIRLING FEEL OR LOOK LIKE TO YOU?

## JESUS HAS OPENED THE HEAVENS

- Through Jesus, we can all find our portals into an open heaven. Jesus has already made the way for us!

- As children of God, we now carry the mandate to open the way for others.

- In Christ, we can find peace, joy, clarity of mind, and divine rest in His presence.

## READ: MARK 1:9–10

- John the Baptist gave firsthand testimony about the event we read about in Mark 1 when he said, *"I saw the Spirit descending from heaven like a dove, **and It abode upon Him**"* (John 1:32).

- As we choose to abide in God's Spirit, we can expect the heavens to remain open over our lives.

### AN OPEN HEAVEN REQUIRES AN OPEN EARTH

- We can choose to live in an open heaven.

- Experiencing an open heaven requires our willingness to be an "open earth."

- If you want to live in the reality of open heavens, begin to declare it over your life. Speak it! Sing it! Prophesy it over yourself and over your family.

### PERCEIVING AN OPEN HEAVEN

- We all resonate with unique vibrational frequencies in the Spirit.

- The way we individually relate to each other and to God is unique.

- When the heavens open over a group, people may perceive different manifestations. Each manifestation is valid, each is distinct, and each must be valued.

### WHIRLWINDS OF POWER

- Those who are accustomed to seeing in the Spirit will often describe their experiences by saying things like:
    - » "I saw a whirlwind."
    - » "There was a flurry of lights moving in energetic circles."
    - » "It seemed like there was a powerful vortex spinning around."

- A power portal forms at the location where the two spiritual currents of heaven and earth find a meeting point.

- A whirlwind is an invitation into heavenly encounters.

- The whirlwind is actually a symbol of the Spirit Himself. The Holy Spirit fills us, surrounds us, and welcomes us into heavenly exploration.

### THE BENEFITS OF AN OPEN HEAVEN

- *"The Lord shall open to you His good treasure, the heaven to give the rain to your land in its season, and to bless all the work of your hand: and you shall lend to many nations, and you shall not borrow"* (Deuteronomy 28:12).

- This one Scripture alone describes several supernatural benefits that may be found awaiting you in an open heaven.

- We must learn how to align ourselves with the will and purpose of God in order to partake of each of these benefits.

### OUR RESPONSE TO AN OPEN HEAVEN

## READ: 2 CORINTHIANS 12:2–4

- When God gives us such experiences, they are either for our own personal betterment or for the overall blessing of the body of Christ. They are never given so that we will feel superior or puffed up.

- The more we encounter Christ in the open heavens, the more humble we should become.

- Sometimes, God will share with you His mysteries in the secret place, and these mysteries must remain hidden in your heart.

- When the heavens are opened, vision follows. When vision is received and acted on, God's people prosper in every way.

## REVIEW QUESTIONS

(Page numbers correspond to the *Power Portals* book.)

1. When power portals open, they extend from the _____ to the _____. (p. 83)

2. How does 2 Chronicles 7:14 speak to your current situation?

   _____

   _____

   _____

   _____

3. Where did King Solomon built the first temple—a location that has become a massive portal? (p. 86)

   _____ _____ _____.

4. People of _____ have created _____ _____ in various places. (p. 86)

5. Every new song from God is intended to take you into a new _____ in Him. (p. 88)

6. Your _____ happens as you _____ with God's truth. (p. 91)

7. What can we learn from Paul's statement that he *"heard unspeakable words, which it is not lawful for a man to utter"* (2 Corinthians 12:4)? (p. 96)

   _____

   _____

   _____

   _____

   _____

## ACTIVATIONS

1. **Spend Time in the Open Heavens with Christ**. This activation can be conducted either alone or in a group setting. Paul encourages us in Colossians 3:1–2:

*Since you have been raised to new life with Christ, set your sights on the realities of heaven, where Christ sits in the place of honor at God's right hand. Think about the things of heaven, not the things of earth.* (NLT)

For this activation, I want to give you an opportunity to encounter the heavenly realm for yourself.

- Find a place where you can lie down comfortably with your eyes closed in the presence of the Lord. You may choose to listen to some "soaking music" while you do this. (I have given some music recommendations at the end of this activation.) Or, you may prefer to rest in an atmosphere of silence. The choice is yours, depending upon your comfort level or what is best for the group setting.

- Once you are settled, I want you to close your eyes and see an image of Jesus in front of you. Initially, this may seem like it's your own imagination, but remember, according to Ephesians 2:6, you are seated in heavenly places, so, from this spiritual posture, it should be a natural thing to see Christ. You can trust the Holy Spirit to open your mind to see into the divine supernatural realities of heaven.

- You may see Jesus's likeness in vivid detail, or His likeness may appear abstract in form, but as you visualize Him before you, appreciate His presence and accept the vision you receive.

- As you focus on Jesus, let all of your natural cares fade away into His loving presence. Relax while sensing the peace and kindness of your personal Lord and Savior, Jesus Christ.

- In this vision, approach the Lord by walking closer and closer to Him. There is no fear, only faith and trust in His eternal goodness.

- What do you see Jesus doing? Some people have seen Him extending His healing hands toward them, and others have felt His loving embrace. Still others dance with Jesus or enjoy the comfort of sitting in His welcoming lap. Whatever you see, appreciate it and receive it as a special gift.

- Now, listen for the words that Jesus wants to express to you. He desires to speak into your heart and tell you something special. What do you hear Him saying?

- At this point, you can ask Jesus to take you to a special place He has prepared for you in heaven. He loves to show you His home because heaven is your home as well! Remain in this posture of open awareness and explore the open heavens with Jesus.

Recommended music for this activation (available on CD or digital download):

- *SpiritSpa* by Joshua Mills
- *SpiritSpa 2* by Joshua Mills
- *Messengers of Fire* by Steve Swanson, JoAnn McFatter, and Steve Mitchell
- *From Heaven* by Kimberly and Alberto Rivera
- *Spirit Songs* by Kimberly and Alberto Rivera

2. **Sing a New Song and Experience a New Glory!** As a personal or group activation, practice singing songs that open the heavens over the atmosphere. Using either a guitar, a piano, or another accessible instrument, find a chord pattern that is easy to sing along to. Once you establish a musical flow, begin singing with it in the Spirit, and then sing with new words. This is how a new song comes to open a new realm.

For example, you could use these simple chords:

G  C  D  C

G  C  D  C

Practice singing in the Spirit with that repetitive chord pattern. And then begin singing the words, "Heaven is open, heaven is open, heaven is open right now." As you do this, you will begin to sense the open heavens all around you. You will discover greater freedom to proclaim the promises of God over your life through song. Feel free to begin adding to the song. You might sing, "Healing is here, healing is here, healing is here right now," or "Miracles are flowing, miracles are flowing, miracles are flowing right now." Sing whatever words the Spirit places into your spirit and enjoy the atmosphere of the open heavens!

# LESSON 5

# SYNCHRONIZING WITH THE SPIRIT

Before you begin this lesson, read chapter 5 of *Power Portals*.

*"In all your ways submit to him, and he will make your paths straight."*
—Proverbs 3:6 (NIV)

## IN ALL YOUR WAYS

- There really is only one way to come into perfect alignment with the Spirit: in *all* your ways submit to Him.

## Q: WHAT DOES IT MEAN TO SUBMIT TO THE SPIRIT? HOW WILL YOU DO THIS IN PRACTICE?

## WE MUST LISTEN AND OBEY

- We must *choose* to make our mind obedient to Christ. (See Romans 8:7.)
- We must *choose* to abide in the Holy Spirit.
- Often, the Spirit will nudge us or speak to us through impressions or heaven-sent thoughts.

## Q: HAVE YOU EVER EXPERIENCED THE LEADING OF THE SPIRIT IN THIS WAY? IF SO, HOW HAS HE GOTTEN YOUR ATTENTION?

- Whenever the Spirit speaks, He is attempting to guide us, instruct us, or get our attention about something for our own good.
- God wants to speak to us about every area of our lives.

## READ: LUKE 5:1–11

- When the Spirit begins to speak, we have a choice to make.

### RESPONDING TO THE SPIRIT REALM

- Your places of disappointment can become places of divine appointment and provision.

Q: ARE YOU WILLING TO BEGIN SYNCHRONIZING WITH THE SPIRIT? IF SO, WHAT ARE SOME AREAS OF YOUR LIFE THAT YOU NEED TO SURRENDER TO GOD AND COMMIT TO HIM?

- Open your ears and heart to hear what the Spirit is speaking to you today, and then respond to Him. Let Him lead and guide you into a life of abundant miracles.

### SYNCHRONIZATION BRINGS HEALTH

- Not everything is beneficial to our physical, emotional, and spiritual health, and we must be conscious of how our attitudes and actions are affecting us.
- *"If you are willing and obedient, you will eat the good things of the land"* (Isaiah 1:19 NIV).
- We must be willing to be taught by the Spirit regarding all matters of life, and we must also be obedient to the Spirit's instruction once we have heard it.
- We must not fight against His flow but, rather, learn how to enter into it with ease.

Q: HOW DO YOU THINK SYNCHRONIZING WITH THE SPIRIT CAN BRING HEALTH?

### HEIGHTENING YOUR SPIRITUAL AWARENESS

- Because our physical body is directly connected to our soul—which is also connected to our spirit—what we eat is important. It not only affects us physically, but it also has long-term spiritual effects.

- When I choose to make wise and healthy decisions concerning nutrition, I've discovered that not only are my mind and body able to operate at a higher capacity of efficiency, but my spirit is also keenly alert to perceive and operate at a higher level of spiritual awareness.

- More importantly, what we spiritually eat affects us physically. It works both ways. We were created as two-way channels for God's presence to continually flow through us.

- The divine impartations that flow into us change us within, whereas the anointing that flows out from us changes the atmosphere around us.

## LEARNING TO DIGEST THE FRUIT OF THE SPIRIT

## READ: GALATIANS 5:22–23

- The *"fruit of the Spirit"* that Paul speaks of in Galatians is actually one fruit.

- Just as our body needs to learn how to adjust to and digest certain nutrients from natural foods, our spirit-man must learn how to fully digest all the nutrients from the fruit of the Spirit.

- Give the Spirit permission to stretch you, grow you, expand your tolerance, and form you in His loving way. Find yourself being encircled by God's living light.

- Don't look at the obstacles ahead of you as a battle. Rather, view them as an opportunity to overcome. Instead of seeing the natural hardships around you as conflicts, see them as "fruit tests" that will make you stronger and healthier.

## Q: HOW HAVE YOU LEARNED TO BETTER DEMONSTRATE THE FRUIT OF THE SPIRIT?

## NO MORE ROOM FOR EXCUSES

- Let me ask you a few questions:
  - » Does God want you to feel weary?
  - » Do you think God desires for you to feel defeated on a daily basis?
  - » Has God called you into an unhealthy lifestyle?
  - » Has heaven run out of provision for your needs?

- Our culture has taught us to make excuses rather than take personal responsibility.

- People made excuses back in Bible times too.

## READ: JOHN 5:2–9

- In John 5, Jesus asked the man with the debilitating condition, *"Do you want to get well?"* But instead of answering with a resounding, "Yes!" he gave Jesus an excuse.

- When the Spirit wants to bring us the blessings of heaven, we need to learn how to receive them. This means stepping out of our comfort zones.

## Q: WHAT ARE SOME COMFORT ZONES IN YOUR LIFE THAT YOU NEED TO STEP OUT OF?

### BEING LED BY THE SPIRIT IN EVERY WAY

- The Scriptures are clear that it is essential for us to be led by the Spirit.

- *"For as many as are led by the Spirit of God, they are the sons of God"* (Romans 8:14).

- When we align with the Spirit, He begins to position us exactly where God wants us to be in life.

- Many birds and animals are led by a type of supernatural sense.

- As believers, we have a similar capability to detect where we should be or where we should go.

- When we are led by the Spirit, we have a strong sense of being drawn in one direction or another when it comes to the situations we face on a day-to-day basis. Such discernment helps us to know:

  » What to do

  » Where to do it

  » How to do it

  » When to do it

- As we grow closer to the Spirit by faith and allow His anointing to flow through us, this spiritual sense becomes more apparent.

- In Acts 20:22, Paul told the Ephesian elders, *"And now, compelled by the Spirit, I am going to Jerusalem, not knowing what will happen to me there"* (NIV).

- We live in the fear, or reverence, of the Lord, which leads us to His peace, direction, and divine spontaneity.

- Through our spirit, we make connections with the spiritual realm.

- Through our soul and with our mind, we operate in the intellectual realm.

- Through our physical body, we make contact with the physical realm.

- If we want to open ourselves to fully receive from God—and, in turn, be used by God to release His power in every sphere of our lives—we must learn how to engage with Him through the portals available to us in our own being—spirit, soul, and body.

- I've identified seven specific personal portals within the human body that should be aligned with the purposes of God. They are:

    1. The heart (spirit)

    2. The mouth

    3. The eyes and ears

    4. The mind

    5. The innermost being

    6. The hands

    7. The feet

- These are not the only portals that exist within us, but they are the seven main openings that we will concentrate on in the course of this study.

# Q: HAVE YOU BECOME AWARE OF THE SPIRITUAL SIGNIFICANCE OF THESE PORTALS? IN WHAT WAYS ARE THEY IMPORTANT TO SYNCHRONIZING WITH THE SPIRIT?

- When I see these particular portals in the Spirit realm, they look like bright whirlwinds to me.

- These portals open within us to receive impartations from the Spirit. We must be willing to receive these gifts, and we must also remain open to release them to others as we continue to synchronize with the Spirit.

# Q: HAVE YOU DISCOVERED OTHER PERSONAL PORTALS WITHIN YOUR BODY? IF SO, WHERE ARE THEY LOCATED AND WHAT IS THEIR SIGNIFICANCE?

## REVIEW QUESTIONS

(Page numbers correspond to the *Power Portals* book.)

1.  *"The carnal mind is _____ against God: for it is not subject to the law of God"* (Romans 8:7). (pp. 97–98)

2.  I believe that God wants to speak to us about every area of our lives, both the _____ things and the _____ things. (p. 99)

3.  In Luke 5:1–11, what was Peter's objection to Jesus's command to launch out his boat into the deep and let down his nets? What happened when he obeyed? What was Peter's response to this miracle? (pp. 99–100)

    _____

    _____

    _____

    _____

    _____

4.  Think of several times when you failed to heed the Spirit's voice. What were the consequences?

    _____

    _____

    _____

    _____

    _____

5.  In the Scriptures, the sin of _____ is listed right alongside the sin of

    _____. (p. 102)

6.  What changes are you ready to make in response to how the Spirit has been speaking to you in this lesson?

    _____

    _____

    _____

7.  Name the seven specific personal portals within the human body that should be aligned with the purposes of God: (p. 111)

    1. _____    5. _____

    2. _____    6. _____

    3. _____    7. _____

    4. _____

## ACTIVATIONS

**Enjoy Healthy and Delicious "Glory Juices"!** For this personal (or group) activation, I want to share two recipes that I use on a regular basis. The first recipe is for Green Glory Smoothie. It's great for your overall health and will give you an energetic start to your mornings! For these recipes, I always recommend using fresh, organic fruits and vegetables.

### GREEN GLORY SMOOTHIE

Makes approximately 78 oz.

1 cucumber

2 handfuls of baby spinach

1 handful of parsley

1 handful of cilantro

3 green apples

a stock of celery (processed through a juicer or strainer)

1 piece fresh turmeric root

1 piece fresh ginger root

1 clove of garlic

a freshly squeezed lemon

a few fresh mint leaves

a dash of cayenne pepper

Puree all ingredients together in a blender, adding high-PH balanced water, according to the desired consistency.

*Nutritional Benefits:* Helps aid in digestion, may boost metabolism, and contains overall natural healing properties.

*Spiritual Benefits:* When used on a daily basis, it has helped me think more clearly and has increased healthy frequencies in my body. (See Genesis 1:29.)

My friend Nichole Lawrence shared the second recipe with me. She is anointed to release "glory sounds" and create spiritual atmospheres through music. Over the past few years, Nichole has been on a nutritional journey with juicing. She encouraged me to partake of Communion using this special Communion Red Juice recipe. It is easy to make, and I have customized it a bit according to my preferences. After I partake of it, it leaves a healthy feeling in my body for several hours.

# COMMUNION RED JUICE

Makes approximately 32 oz.

6 apples

1 beet (processed through a juicer or strainer)

1 peeled lime

1 pint raspberries

1 cluster of red grapes

Puree all ingredients together in a blender. Serve in small Communion cups along with your choice of unleavened bread. (I recommend using cut squares of coconut wrap.)

*Nutritional Benefits*: High in antioxidants. Purifies the blood.

*Spiritual Benefits*: Aids in drawing closer to Christ, in healing, and in receiving forgiveness. (See Leviticus 17:11; Luke 22:20.)

When using this juice for Communion, you may want to listen to Nicole Lawrence's anointed music. Dr. David Van Koevering has said, "This music is the result of being directed completely by the Holy Spirit. The result has demonstrated healing of lung issues, multiple sclerosis, shaking from palsy, blood issues, spiritual issues of depression, and fear."

Recommended music for this activation (available on CD and digital download):

*Receive Your Healing* by Joshua Mills and Steve Swanson

*Healing Glory* by Nichole Lawrence

# LESSON 6

# THE SEVEN DIMENSIONS OF DIVINE POWER

Before you begin this lesson, read chapter 6 of *Power Portals*.

*"The kingdom of God has come with power."*
—Mark 9:1 (NIV)

## PORTALS OF POWER

- A helpful way to understand portals is to think of them as sending and receiving centers for God's power to be released to you and through you.

- There is always a flow of great power when God's Spirit moves in our lives.

- Not only do we have seven personal portals through which the Spirit can move, but the Spirit has seven dimensions of divine power through which He manifests His works.

## GREATER GROWTH IS NEEDED FOR GREATER POWER

- When we yield to God, He increases His power in us.

- We experience the power of God in degrees:

    » From faith to faith

    » From strength to strength

    » From glory to glory

- God doesn't deposit all of His power into our lives at one time or else we would surely die.

- We need greater spiritual growth to be able to handle greater degrees of His power.

### THE SEVEN DIMENSIONS

- Each dimension of divine power builds upon the previous one, so that, as we grow spiritually and enter into all these dimensions, we will ultimately know how to reach the highest level of power available to mankind.

## READ: EPHESIANS 1:18–23

- Within Ephesians 1:18–23 alone, we find five of the seven Greek words for God's power that we will be reviewing in this study.

- You can tap into all these dimensions so that God's transforming power may flow through you as you awaken your connection to the Spirit realm.

### FIRST DIMENSION: ISCHYS—FORCEFUL POWER

## READ: MARK 12:30

- The Greek word for *"strength"* in Mark 12:30 is *ischys*. Among its meanings are "forcefulness," "ability," "might," "power," and "strength." (*Strong's*, #G2479)

- *Ischys* is God's resident power in the life of a believer, the working power of the Spirit within us.

- This power must be directed back toward heaven in a supernatural cycle, from God and for God.

- The power has nothing to do with us, except that we must be willing to submit to it.

- We are conduits of God's power.

# Q: WHAT DOES IT MEAN TO BE A SPIRITUAL CONDUIT? HAVE YOU EVER EXPERIENCED GOD'S POWER IN THIS WAY?

- When you remain connected to Jesus, the power flows.

- *"Finally, my brethren, be strong in the Lord, and in the power of His might [ischys]"* (Ephesians 6:10).

- *Ischys* is the power of the Spirit that is connected to prayer, fasting, and a lifestyle of devotion.

- When dealing with evil spirits, we must remember what Jesus told His disciples after He cast out a demon that was entrenched in a young boy when they had been unable to do so.

1. He told them they lacked faith.

2. He added, *"However this kind goes not out but by prayer and fasting"* (Matthew 17:21).

- Jesus was emphasizing that we need to build ourselves up spiritually and continually be in a right relationship with Jesus Christ in order to effectively minister deliverance.

- If we want to witness a greater release of *ischys* power, we must surrender to the work of the Spirit and allow Him to make the changes that are required for the betterment of our lives and the effectiveness of our ministry.

### SECOND DIMENSION: KRATOS—PREVAILING POWER

## READ: EPHESIANS 3:16

- The Greek term translated *"strengthened"* in Ephesians 3:16 comes from the root word *kratos*. Among its meanings are "vigor," "dominion," "might," "power," and "strength." (*Strong's*, #G2904)

- This dimension of God's power is given to us by the Spirit for our inner man.

- It builds us up inwardly so we can manifest His strength outwardly.

- Faith is the dominant factor involved in this dimension.

- *Kratos* power is given to us so that we can be overcomers regardless of the situation we may be facing.

- When both *kratos* and *ischys* dimensions begin operating in your life, it releases the supernatural energy of God.

### THIRD DIMENSION: ENERGIA AND ENERGEŌ—ENERGIZING POWER

## READ: EPHESIANS 3:7

- The Greek word *energeia* used in Ephesians 3:7 quite simply means "[divine] energy." (*Strong's*, #G1754)

- This is the level of power that supernaturally enables us to work actively and efficiently.

- Divine energy is the strength and vitality that's required for sustained spiritual activity, as well as for physical and mental endeavors.

- Everything that comes from God is for the whole person.

- Divine energy is given to us so that we can effectively do whatever God has called us to do.

## Q: IN WHAT AREAS OF YOUR PERSONAL LIFE DO YOU NEED AN INCREASE OF DIVINE ENERGY TO FLOW?

### FOURTH DIMENSION: DYNAMIS—MIRACULOUS POWER

- Jesus said, *"You will receive power when the Holy Spirit comes on you; and you will be my witnesses"* (Acts 1:8 NIV).

- The Greek word translated *"power"* here is *dynamis*. (*Strong's*, #G1411)

- It is supernatural dynamite—explosive power!

- This dimension of power signifies there is nothing in the natural that can block what God has for us in the Spirit.

- Such power is for those who *believe*—and this is key.

- The kingdom of God is a realm of real power.

- We cannot work miracles through human efforts, abilities, natural talents, or self-power.

- Jesus said, *"Without Me you can do nothing"* (John 15:5).

- Miracles flow from and through a genuine relationship with Jesus Christ.

## Q: HOW HAVE YOU EXPERIENCED *DYNAMIS* POWER WORKING IN YOUR LIFE?

### FIFTH DIMENSION: EXOUSIA—AUTHORITATIVE POWER

## READ: MATTHEW 10:1; 28:18

- The Greek word translated *"power"* in Matthew 10:1 and Matthew 28:18 is *exousia*, which can variously mean "delegated influence," "authority," "jurisdiction," "liberty," "power," "right," and "strength." (*Strong's*, #G1849)

- Jesus gave His disciples *exousia* power to proclaim the Word, cast out demons, and heal the sick.

## Q: ARE YOU A DISCIPLE OF CHRIST? IF SO, DO YOU BELIEVE THAT HE HAS TRULY GIVEN YOU *EXOUSIA* POWER?

- *"But as many as received Him, to them gave He power [exousia] to become the sons of God, even to them that believe on His name"* (John 1:12).

# Q: WHAT ARE SOME OF THE WAYS THAT WE CAN TAKE SPIRITUAL AUTHORITY THROUGH THIS POWER OF GOD?

- Christians have the *exousia*, or authority, to convey the power of God's Spirit through the laying on of hands.

- *Exousia* can be imparted from the portals of your hands.

- The hands are spiritual touch points used to release God's power.

### SIXTH DIMENSION: HARPAZŌ—DELIVERANCE POWER

## READ: MATTHEW 11:12

- The Greek word translated *"force"* in Matthew 11:12 is *harpazō*. Among its meanings are "to seize," "to catch up," "to pluck," "to pull," and "to take by force." (*Strong's*, #G726)

- Both Philip and the apostle Paul experienced *harpazō* power. (See Acts 8:39; 2 Corinthians 12:2.)

- When *harpazō* power is working in your life, it will allow you to receive divine insight regarding ministry assignments, and, at times, it will provide a supernatural portal of access to them.

- When *harpazō* power comes upon us, it literally snatches us up in an instant to be transported into the purposes of God.

# Q: HAVE YOU EVER EXPERIENCED BEING "CAUGHT UP" BY THIS LEVEL OF GOD'S POWER? HAVE YOU HEARD OF OTHERS EXPERIENCING THIS SUPERNATURAL DIMENSION? HOW DO YOU SEE GOD USING THIS LEVEL OF POWER IN YOUR LIFE?

- I believe the Spirit wants you to experience this level of His supernatural power more and more.

### SEVENTH DIMENSION: ESPIKIAZŌ—OVERSHADOWING POWER

- This seventh dimension is the highest power of God available to mankind, and it is connected to the glory realm.

- The Greek word *espikiazō* means "to cast a shade upon," "to envelop in a haze of brilliancy," and "to invest with preternatural influence." (*Strong's*, #G1982)

- This dimension of divine power functions like a New Testament cloud of glory in that it expands within an atmosphere, touching those who are within its reach.

READ: ACTS 5:15

- Peter carried this power. It was the atmosphere of God's power upon Peter's life that caused the sick to be healed everywhere he went.

Q: HAVE YOU EVER FELT A SHIFT IN THE ATMOSPHERE WHEN YOU WERE AROUND SOMEONE WHO HAD SPENT TIME IN THE PRESENCE OF THE LORD? HOW DID IT MAKE YOU FEEL? DID YOU NOTICE ANY SUBTLE CHANGES OR VISIBLE RESULTS?

- The atmosphere of *episkiazō* can envelop any disease and bring life and healing to any situation.
- The overshadowing *"power of the Highest"* (Luke 1:35) is available for you to access today.

## REVIEW QUESTIONS

(Page numbers correspond to the *Power Portals* book.)

Below, name the seven dimensions of God's power and give a brief definition and an example of each:

1. First dimension: (pp. 118–120)

   _____

   _____

   _____

   _____

   _____

2. Second dimension: (pp. 120–121)

   _____

   _____

   _____

   _____

   _____

3. Third dimension: (pp. 121–123)

   _____

   _____

   _____

   _____

   _____

4. Fourth dimension: (pp. 123–125)

   _____

   _____

   _____

   _____

   _____

5. Fifth dimension: (pp. 125–128)

   _____

   _____

   _____

   _____

   _____

6.  Sixth dimension: (pp. 128–129)

 

 

 

 

 

7.  Seventh dimension: (pp. 129–130)

 

 

 

 

 

## ACTIVATIONS

1. **Power in Your Hands!** This activation is for either personal or group application. You will invite the Holy Spirit to manifest His *energeia* power between the palms of your hands. In this way, you will be aware of it and willing to release it to others. Remember, your hands are one of the spiritual touch points through which God chooses to release His power.

- Let's start with a prayer:

    Father, in the name of Jesus, I thank You for the power of Your Spirit, which flows through me completely. I ask You to cause Your *energeia* to flow up from my innermost being, down through my arms, and into the palms of my hands. I choose to be a releaser of the power that You have given me. I will lay hands on the sick and see them recover. I will lay hands on those who desire to receive a fresh impartation and see them excel. I will lay hands on those who are oppressed and see them set free by the power of Your Spirit. Let Your power flow through me. In Jesus's name, amen!

- Now that you have prayed and invited the power of the Holy Spirit to flow through your body, stand up and raise your arms, with both of your hands out in front of you, palms facing each other, approximately twelve inches apart.

- Close your eyes and concentrate on the power of God that is flowing from your innermost being, up through your arms, and down into your hands. You may quietly pray in tongues or remain silent as you focus on God's *energeia* power flowing through you.

- Next, begin to slowly move the palms of your hands toward each other. As you do this, you will begin to feel a slight resistance. To me, it often feels like a magnetic resistance. This is the flow of God's power that is being released between the palms of your hands. Don't push through this feeling. Rather, begin to lightly embrace it with your hands. At this point, you may begin to sense an electrical tingling sensation in your palms or fingertips. Thank the Spirit for allowing you to sense His power. You are detecting the *energeia* of God.

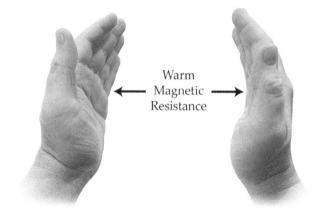

- As you continue to thank the Lord and recognize His *energeia* power flowing through you, ask Him for what purpose this power is being given to you. He may tell you that it's a healing flow, an impartation of some sort, or for the resolution of a specific situation. If you are directed to naturally release this power to someone else in the room, do so, but first ask their permission. If God shows you a need that seems out of reach, release this power into that situation by the Spirit.

- In a group setting, you can share testimonies of your experiences. If you have done this activation privately, then journal your experience and prayerfully ask the Spirit how you might utilize this activation the next time you meet someone in need.

2. **Coronation Day.** You will receive a fresh anointing of *exousia* power through this group activation, recognizing that believers have been made *"unto our God kings and priests"* (Revelation 5:10 KJV). In advance, prepare a sacred anointing oil to be used for anointing the heads of those participating (for a recipe, see page 150 of *Power Portals*). Review the significance of this ceremony from pages 127–128 of *Power Portals* and utilize the prayer on page 128, speaking aloud the blessing over those whom you anoint.

3. **Overshadowing Power.** Through this study, you've learned that God's *episkiazō* power comes to overshadow you with His goodness. This power can be tangibly felt in the atmosphere and flows with an abundance of miracles. In this activation, which is appropriate for either personal and group application, you will invite the Holy Spirit to introduce you to this level of His power so that you might be a carrier and releaser of *episkiazō* everywhere you go!

- Again, let's start with a prayer:

  Father, in the name of Jesus, I thank You for Your *episkiazō* power, which overshadows me with Your goodness and glory. I desire to know You in a greater way and to carry Your knowledge and power to everyone I meet. Right now, I ask You to cover me with the weight of Your power and bring glory to Your name. Let Your power flow over me and through me. In Jesus's name, amen!

- Now, with your eyes closed so that you can focus on these spiritual realities, begin lifting your hands as if you were receiving a gift from heaven (which you are!).

- As you lift your hands and welcome God's Spirit in this way, you will begin to notice the "weightiness" of His power coming upon you. It may be lighter at first and then gradually intensify as you focus on what the Holy Spirit is doing through you. You may begin to feel a gentle weight upon your forehead, your shoulders, or the open palms of your hands. Sometimes, people describe a feeling like the pressure (though not uncomfortable) of a large hand resting on their chest or back. This is the hand of God, the glory of His presence, ministering to you in a powerful way. Receive and rest in the imparta-tions that come with *episkiazō* power. Begin to learn how to live in this dimension. God wants you to be a carrier of His goodness everywhere you go!

# PART III
# ACTIVATING POWER PORTALS

# LESSON 7

# OPENING PERSONAL PORTALS

Before you begin this lesson, read chapter 7 of *Power Portals*.

*"Don't you realize that your body is the temple of the Holy Spirit, who lives in you and was given to you by God? You do not belong to yourself."*
—1 Corinthians 6:19 (NLT)

- You are a temple in which the Spirit of the living God dwells, and this temple has many "doors" connected with the spiritual realm.

## READ: PSALM 24:9–10

- Jesus is the King of Glory.

- We are the *"ancient gates"* that must be opened.

- While Jesus is our portal into heavenly glory, we can become His portals, bringing heavenly glory into the earth.

- We go in through Him, and He pours out through us by His Spirit.

## HOW OUR PERSONAL PORTALS CONNECT

- Within our body, we have been provided with many "doors." As mentioned in an earlier lesson, these personal portals are:

  1. The heart (spirit)

  2. The mouth

  3. The eyes and ears

  4. The mind

5. The innermost being

6. The hands

7. The feet

- All of our personal portals are connected to each other in some form.

- The heart is connected to the mouth. (See Luke 6:45.)

- The mouth is connected to the eyes and ears. (See Romans 10:17.)

- The eyes and ears are connected to the mind. (See Matthew 13:16; 2 Corinthians 4:18.)

- The mind is connected to the innermost being. (See Philippians 4:8; John 7:38.)

- The innermost being is connected to the hands and feet. (See Psalm 63:4; Psalm 37:23.)

- We are fully awakened when we make connections with the Spirit realm through our personal power portals.

- The Spirit desires to flow through every open pathway that we submit to Him.

## THE HEART

- Your heart is a portal for eternity.

- Every miracle begins in the heart of God, and He desires to transfer it to us—heart-to-heart—in a very special way.

- *"Look! I stand at the door and knock. If you hear my voice and open the door, I will come in, and we will share a meal together as friends"* (Revelation 3:20 NLT).

- The Holy Spirit finds entrance through an open and willing heart.

- Just as Jesus was the temple of God's Spirit on earth, we become temples of the Spirit to the world around us.

- The portal of your heart sets the atmosphere for each and every one of your other portals.

- If we set our heart right, we will set our life right.

- Thanksgiving becomes a spiritual vortex that draws the blessings of heaven toward us.

- The spirit of this world is dark and cold, but when you have a thankful heart, you become bright and warm. You shine with the radiance of gratefulness!

- *"For God, who commanded the light to shine out of darkness, has shined in our hearts, to give the light of the knowledge of the glory of God in the face of Jesus Christ"* (2 Corinthians 4:6).

## THE MOUTH

READ: LUKE 6:45

- Your mouth is a portal for both receiving and releasing the blessing.

- *"Set a watch, O LORD, before my mouth; keep the door of my lips"* (Psalm 141:3).

- David was a man of worship, and yet he needed God to guard his mouth.

- The mouth is a doorway in and a doorway out.

- This portal was created by God to be a source of life.

- In the natural, the mouth is a place to receive healthy nutrition.

- In the realm of the Spirit, it is the place to release spiritual nourishment to others.

- God's temple must be honored. "I honor God's temple because I honor God."

## Q: WHAT DOES THIS SAYING MEAN TO YOU? IN WHAT PRACTICAL WAYS CAN YOU HONOR GOD'S TEMPLE?

- "Let words be thy medicine, and let medicine be thy words."

- The words we speak have the ability to either condemn us or bless us.

- Just like a portal, our words create pathways for either bad conditions or heavenly conditions to enter our lives.

- Speaking God's words releases freedom, healing, joy, peace, pleasure, and the life of the Spirit.

- Look at the statements on page 146 of *Power Portals* and examine the ways in which God wants to give you a new glory vocabulary.

- You can trust that God will give you even more new ways to speak so that your uncommon words are transformed into uncommon blessings!

## THE EYES AND EARS

- Your eyes and ears are portals of purity and faith.

READ: MATTHEW 13:15–17

# Q: WHAT WAS JESUS SPEAKING ABOUT IN THIS PASSAGE? WHY SHOULD WE OPEN OUR EYES AND EARS?

- Let's focus on the eyes first because the eyes are the window to the soul.

- The pupils are quite literally portal openings into the eyes.

- *"When your eye is healthy, your whole body is filled with light. But when it is unhealthy, your body is filled with darkness"* (Luke 11:34 NLT).

- Our eyes are so powerful that whatever we focus on will become magnified in our lives. This happens to us both physically and spiritually.

- This power portal also includes our ears: *"Faith comes by hearing, and hearing by the word of God"* (Romans 10:17).

- Good hearing is essential to our physical and emotional well-being.

- As portals, your ears are divinely suited to hear the spoken Word of God.

- If you hear the Word over and over, you will be focused to do what it says.

## THE MIND

- Your mind is a portal for godly wisdom.

## READ: ROMANS 12:2

- The Spirit desires to touch your mind with His glory.

- When we are mindful of the Lord, we are more fully present with Him.

# Q: TO WHAT DO YOU GIVE YOUR ATTENTION? WHAT HAS YOUR MIND BEEN FOCUSING ON?

- The Spirit reveals to us the truth about Himself and also about ourselves. He will show us the thoughts and attitudes we have held on to that need to be removed from our lives and done away with forever.

- The first step to taking authority over harmful mindsets is to reject them while forgiving yourself for believing such harmful ideas in the first place.

- The next step is to forgive those who originally "gifted" you with those thoughts. Many of our negative thought patterns have been handed down to us from previous generations.

- Harmful mindsets are filled with ideas from the enemy that have invaded our souls with their dark spiritual vibrations.

- If we're living pure before the Lord, these thoughts have no real substance in us and do not belong to us as believers. (See Galatians 3:13–14.)

- Your mind is a power portal that should be illuminated by Christ's thoughts.

- *"'Who can know the Lord's thoughts? Who knows enough to teach him?' But we understand these things, for we have the mind of Christ"* (1 Corinthians 2:16 NLT).

- Make the following declaration:

  > My personal portals are precious. They are doorways into and out of God's temple. They are holy. I will stand guard over them.

## THE INNERMOST BEING

- Your innermost being is a portal for discernment and sacred spontaneity.

## READ: EPHESIANS 3:16–19

- This portal is located around your stomach area, down in your gut.

- This is the location where most of your spiritual hunger and discernment are released.

- Your innermost being is also where you receive and carry the infilling of the Holy Spirit.

- This portal activates your mouth to speak in heavenly languages through the release that comes from your innermost being.

- There is much overlap in your personal portals when you are filled with the Spirit, and this is the way God intended it to be. He wants you to be filled to overflowing!

- Your heart (which is the seat of your spirit) and your innermost being (which is the seat of your soul) cover a wide spiritual expanse. This is your spiritual core.

- *"He that believes on Me, as the scripture has said, out of his belly* [innermost being] *shall flow rivers of living water"* (John 7:38).

- This flow is not something to be frightened of; it should be embraced and released as a mighty rushing river.

- David wrote, *"O Lord, hear me as I pray; pay attention to my groaning"* (Psalm 5:1 NLT).

- Open up this portal, and let the sound come forth!

- When God is bringing about a deep emotional or spiritual healing in you, you may feel a fire within your stomach area. This is the work of the Holy Spirit within you.

- It is common for people to feel, coming from this same physical area, a strong compulsion to pray and seek the Lord.

- In Luke 22:44, Jesus *"prayed more earnestly."*

- This type of deep prayer is called *"the bowels of compassion"* (1 John 3:17). (See Genesis 43:30.)

## Q: HAVE YOU EVER EXPERIENCED THIS TYPE OF DEEP AND INTENSE PRAYER, WHICH COMES FROM YOUR INNERMOST BEING? IF SO, WHAT WAS THE END RESULT?

- Within Solomon's temple, the holiest part was also called the *"oracle"* because it was the place where God would speak to His people. (See 1 Kings 6:16, 19.)

- There is also an "oracle" within you. Your innermost being is the place where you can hear, recognize, and connect to the voice of God that is speaking clearly to you.

- Some people call this their "gut instinct." (See Psalm 16:7.)

- From your innermost being, you will receive supernatural insight, discernment, clarity, and a great surge of power for moving forward into your God-appointed destiny.

### THE HANDS

- Your hands are portals of power and prosperity

- Jesus said, *"They shall lay hands on the sick, and they shall recover"* (Mark 16:18).

- There is heavenly power in your hands!

- The Spirit wants to work various types of miracles through the power portals of our hands, but we must be willing to extend our hands toward people and places in need.

- It is important for you to understand that your hands are the portals from which miraculous power flows. Look at the statements below and write corresponding Scripture references underneath each one (see pp. 158–159 in the *Power Portals* book):

1. Your hands release the works of God's power.

   _____

   _____

2. Your hands release the healing virtue of Jesus Christ.

   _____

   _____

3. Your hands are signs of blessing.

   _____

   _____

4. Your hands are filled with prosperity.

   _____

   _____

5. Your hands symbolize long life and eternal pleasure.

   _____

   _____

- When you stretch out your hands in faith, don't do it in a casual way. Do it with intention.
- Very often, I see the power of the Spirit—flowing up from the portal of my innermost being into my arms and then continuing down through my wrists and out through my open hands—as a golden current of power.
- This power comes from heaven, but it flows through me.
- Our hands are the place where heaven is released in a very tangible way.

Q: HOW HAVE YOU SEEN GOD WORK MIRACLES THROUGH YOUR HANDS? IF YOU HAVEN'T YET EXPERIENCED THIS MINISTRY, HOW WILL YOU BEGIN OPENING THE POWER PORTALS OF YOUR HANDS TO RELEASE MIRACLES?

## THE FEET

- Your feet are portals of possession.

READ: JOSHUA 1:3

- Every location where you put your feet becomes a new place that you can take authority over for the glory of God.

- Learn how to pray as you walk. When you do this, God will begin to bring you divine insight. You can trust that His Spirit will reveal both the spiritual root problems and the divine solutions that are needed in any particular area in order to bring transformation to that place or situation.

- If you let the Spirit direct your steps, you will be amazed at the places and opportunities to which He leads you.

- As the portal of your feet is opened to claim new places for God's purpose, favor will become your footstep! (See Job 29:6.)

## CLEANSING YOUR PORTALS

- Spend a few moments in honest reflection about ways in which you may have dishonored God through your portals. For example: using your heart to worship vain idols; using your eyes to watch unclean movies; using your ears to listen to harmful ideas; using your mind to think devious thoughts; using your innermost being to ignore the voice of the Holy Spirit; using your hands to type gossip or steal from others; using your feet to go into prohibited places.

- True and lasting change can only begin with authentic repentance, prayer, and seeking after God.

- Private prayer results in public power.

- Take time to pray over each personal portal in your physical body. Looking at the chart on page 160 in *Power Portals*, begin anointing your various personal portals while using the recommended decrees.

## REVIEW QUESTIONS

(Page numbers correspond to the *Power Portals* book.)

1.  List a few of the most important issues of the heart and God's answer to them: (p. 140)

    _____

    _____

    _____

    _____

    _____

2.  What are some things you used to say that you now realize you must change in order to align your words with God's Word? And what are some of the new phrases you will say? (Feel free to reference p. 146.)

    _____

    _____

    _____

    _____

    _____

3.  What mixture of essential oils did I recommend using for anointing the portals of your eyes and ears? (p. 147)

    _____

    _____

    _____

    _____

    _____

4.  While studying about the portal of the mind, did the Spirit bring to your memory some previously hidden thoughts that need to change? If so, list them, along with a promise from God's Word that brings light.

    _____

    _____

    _____

    _____

    _____

5.  Jesus said, *"He that believes on Me, as the scripture has said, out of his* _____
    [_____ _____] *shall flow rivers of living water"* (John 7:38). (p. 154)

6. Our hands receive _____ and our hands give _____. Prosperity comes to our lives through our hands, and we have the _____ of letting prosperity _____ to others through those same hands. (pp. 160–161)

7. What is the purpose of the portal of your feet? (p. 161)

_____

_____

_____

_____

_____

## ACTIVATIONS

1. **You Are a Power Portal!** Using the chart below, write down the specific portals and what God is personally speaking to you about each one. Add Scriptures that resonate with you and any details that might be helpful for keeping your portals open to receive and give from the Spirit. Include any thoughts the Spirit has spoken to you concerning your portals during this study.

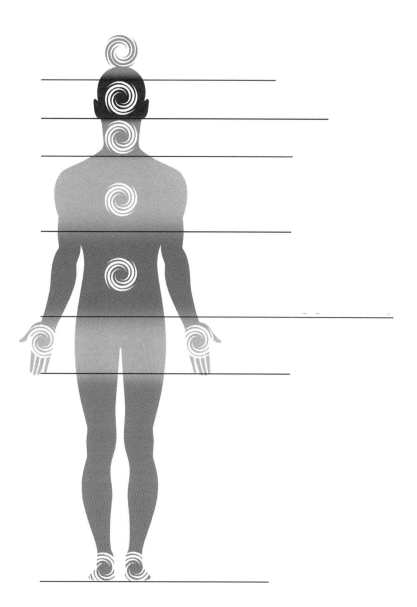

2. **A Prayer for Having a "God" Day**. Instead of just having a good day, the Spirit wants you to have a "God" day! A God day is filled with supernatural "suddenlys" and is overflowing with heaven's blessings! Because you are a power portal, God wants you to shine His light everywhere you go. When Janet and I take our daughters to school, we always remind them, "Have a God day, and give a God day!" Here is a simple prayer that you can begin praying on a daily basis to ensure that your portals are positioned for blessing:

Dear Lord,

| | |
|---|---|
| Here is my heart…. | Love through it. |
| Here is my mouth…. | Speak through it. |
| Here are my eyes and ears…. | See and listen through them. |
| Here is my mind…. | Think through it. |
| Here is my innermost being…. | Flow through it. |
| Here are my hands…. | Touch with them. |
| Here are my feet…. | Walk with them. |
| Here am I…. | Shine Your light through me. |

Amen.

3. **Speak in the New Way!** Using the chart on page 146 of *Power Portals* as a launching board, consider changing some of your vocabulary by speaking in a new way, as discussed in this study and in the Review Questions. You can pick one phrase and practice using it! Also, the Spirit may speak to you very personally about some of the words you've been using, words that He would like to change. Write them down here as a helpful reminder. As the Spirit gives you new words to say, write the new words next to the old ones.

_____

_____

_____

_____

_____

_____

_____

_____

_____

_____

_____

4. **What Do You Have in Your Hands?** As a personal activation, take a moment to look at the chart below. It details many different types of blessings that God is able to cause to flow from your hands.

Recognize that God's power is not only available to you, but it is also accessible to flow through your hands to others by the work of the Holy Spirit. Now, place your hands in an open position in front of you (as though you were receiving a gift) and look at them. Instead of just seeing them as you have in the past, ask God to reveal to you what kinds of spiritual blessings and powerful impartations He has placed within your hands. Write down what the Spirit reveals to you and the ways in which you will choose to steward these blessings and impartations:

_____

_____

_____

_____

_____

_____

_____

_____

_____

_____

_____

_____

_____

_____

# CREATING SPIRITUAL PATHWAYS

Before you begin this lesson, read chapter 8 of *Power Portals*.

*"The testimony of Jesus is the spirit of prophecy."*
—Revelation 19:10

- God has given you a testimony of how He has redeemed you and worked in your life.

- Your testimony is supernatural and potent.

- Your testimony creates pathways in the Spirit realm for others to travel.

- What God has done in your life *is* significant.

## THE PROPHETIC TESTIMONY OF JESUS

- When you share your God-given testimony, it is prophetic in nature. Every time you speak about what God has done for you in the past, you are prophesying over your future as well.

- Focus on your breakthroughs. Faith builds a faith realm.

- In this way, you will open a very wide door in the Spirit to enter into more of the same and invite others to enter as well.

- If someone else received a great blessing, and they're sharing the story about what God has done for them, your response should be rejoicing, just as if the same had happened to you.

- A testimony is a portal, and when it opens, all you need to do is step through it.

- Your agreement takes you all the way into that portal.

- Reach into that portal and pull the spiritual realities that exist there down into your own personal life.
- This is a supernatural transaction.
- Submission to the Lord is the key.

## THE GREATER THINGS

### READ: ROMANS 8:14–17

# Q: WHAT DOES THIS SCRIPTURE PASSAGE MEAN TO YOU?

- We are joint-heirs with Christ, joint-heirs of the greater heavenly things.
- *"For the Father loves the Son and shows him all he does. Yes, and he will show him even greater works than these, so that you will be amazed"* (John 5:20 NIV).
- The Bible says that God the Father showed His Son greater things because He loved Him.
- We are joint-heirs in receiving the greater things that have been promised.
- Jesus said, *"Verily, verily, I say to you, he that believes on Me, the works that I do shall he do also; and greater works than these shall he do; because I go to My Father"* (John 14:12).
- God is bringing us into the greater works!
- Sometimes *good* potential is blocking us from *greater* potential.
- You were created for greatness.

## FOUR PORTALS FOR YOUR TESTIMONY

- Here are four portals that can be opened through your testimony:
    1. A portal of victory
    2. A portal of blessing
    3. A portal of prophetic decree
    4. A portal of creative miracles

### A PORTAL OF VICTORY

- It is important to declare your testimony boldly and allow it to move you past any earthly fears.
- Through your testimony, word by word, brick by brick, you build a pathway for someone else to travel down.

- We give because He first gave to us. (See John 3:16.)

- If God is doing something new through you, it is important for you to share it.

- Share your testimony through the guidance of the Spirit and in the light of His Word.

## Q: WHAT DOES THE ABOVE STATEMENT MEAN TO YOU? HOW CAN YOU SHARE YOUR TESTIMONY IN LIGHT OF GOD'S WORD?

- Your testimony has the ability to create a ladder between earth and heaven, and as you climb it, you can access the victorious riches of God.

- You must declare your testimony because others are waiting to hear it.

- If you fail to share it, you are blocking a realm of victory that was intended for you. In this case, the enemy attempts to "block your blessing" by influencing you to keep your mouth shut.

- On this side of the portal, you may have only one testimony, but when you open the door of your mouth and give forth the good news of what God has done for you, a multiplication takes place in the Spirit realm that moves from heaven to earth.

### A PORTAL OF BLESSING

## READ: PROVERBS 6:2

- You can be ensnared by the words of your mouth—but you can also overcome by the words of your mouth.

- What you receive depends on what you say.

- Jesus said, *"For of the abundance of the heart* [the] *mouth speaks"* (Luke 6:45).

- This is the reason why we must guard the door of our heart (see Proverbs 4:23) and the door of our mouth (see Proverbs 21:23; Psalm 39:1).

- These double doors open for either blessing or cursing.

- There is a very real war going on in the supernatural realm, a war over your testimony.

- *"Greater is He that is in you, than he that is in the world"* (1 John 4:4).

- Here are the two participants in the warfare being fought over your testimony:

1. *"He that is in you"*

2. *"he that is in the world"*

- Let Him who is in you, the Greater One who has taken up residence inside you, shine forth. Let Him be heard! Let Him be seen! Let Him be declared through your testimony!

- When we share our testimony about what God has done for us, His blessings will manifest—even in our physical body.

## A PORTAL OF PROPHETIC DECREE

- Your testimony creates a prophetic pathway in the Spirit.

- Your testimony contains the power to reproduce itself.

- If God has done something for one person, He will do it for another.

- Your testimony is the prophetic pathway that leads others into the supernatural ability of God.

- *"You shall also decree a thing, and it shall be established to you: and the light shall shine upon your ways"* (Job 22:28).

Q: HAVE YOU EVER WITNESSED SOMEONE COMING INTO THE SAME BLESSINGS THAT YOU'VE EXPERIENCED (FOR EXAMPLE, SALVATION, HEALING, OR DELIVERANCE) AFTER YOU'VE SHARED YOUR TESTIMONY? IF NOT, DETERMINE TO SHARE YOUR TESTIMONY TODAY, AND SEE WHAT GOD WILL DO!

## A PORTAL OF CREATIVE MIRACLES

- The more we talk about God's signs and wonders, the more they begin to manifest.

- Your testimony can lay a foundation and create a pathway for creative miracles.

- *"By the word* [or the testimony] *of the Lord were the heavens made; and all the host of them by the breath* [or the vapor] *of His mouth"* (Psalm 33:6).

- The stars and planets, all the hosts of the heavens, were not created from what may be seen; they were created from what is invisible and eternal.

READ: HEBREWS 11:1–3

- Everything in creation that we see right now literally emanated from the word of God. It was all made from His testimony. Think about that!

- Your God-given testimony contains the power to cause what does not exist in the physical world to come into existence.

## THE GLORY ATMOSPHERE CREATES POSSIBILITY

- At the same time God said, *"Let there be light"* (Genesis 1:3), something else was happening in the atmosphere.

- The Spirit of God (or the Spirit of Glory) was hovering over the surface of the deep. (See Genesis 1:2.)

- That was the right condition for the miraculous to manifest.

- God prepares the right condition for your testimony to be spoken by permeating the environment with His presence.

- When we usher in the glory of God, it creates an atmosphere in which we can make our declaration, and instantly the pathways of our spoken words connect to heavenly portals, and blessings easily begin to flow.

## YOUR LIVING TESTIMONY

- The way you live your life is a powerful testimony in itself.

- Your actions should always reinforce the positive words you have spoken.

- I don't want to live my life just trying to make it into heaven; I want to live my life in a way that invites heaven to make itself at home in me.

- It's important to live our lives as an example for others.

- No, we're not perfect. Yet, by God's grace, the Spirit gently speaks to us about necessary changes we must make as we choose to follow Him further on this spiritual path.

- Give the Spirit permission to minister to you about areas in your life that may need to change.

- Jesus said, *"For to whomsoever much is given, of him shall be much required"* (Luke 12:48).

- What we give up in the natural cannot even compare to what we are being entrusted with in the Spirit.

- Live your testimony out loud. Let others see it, hear it, and follow your example into an open portal of heaven's blessing.

## REVIEW QUESTIONS

(Page numbers correspond to the *Power Portals* book.)

1.  What is a testimony? (p. 167)

    _____

    _____

    _____

    _____

    _____

2.  Have you been hesitant to share your testimony? Why or why not?

    _____

    _____

    _____

    _____

    _____

3.  How might you position yourself to receive what another believer is testifying of? (p. 170)

    _____

    _____

    _____

    _____

    _____

4.  What does Revelation 12:11 reveal? (p. 174)

    _____

    _____

    _____

    _____

    _____

5.  Name the four portals that can be opened through your testimony: (p. 174)

    1. _____

    2. _____

    3. _____

    4. _____

6.  In Philippians 4:8, what types of things did Paul admonish us to think on? (p. 177)

    _____

    _____

    _____

    _____

    _____

7.  What do you believe Paul meant when he said, *"All things are lawful for me, but not all things are helpful; all things are lawful for me, but not all things edify"* (1 Corinthians 10:23 NKJV)?

    _____

    _____

    _____

    _____

    _____

## ACTIVATIONS

1. **What Has God Done for You This Week?** Take some time to write a short testimony about the way you've seen the Spirit move in your life this week.

_____

_____

_____

_____

_____

_____

_____

_____

_____

_____

_____

_____

_____

_____

_____

_____

_____

_____

_____

_____

_____

_____

_____

_____

_____

_____

_____

_____

_____

_____

_____

2. **Start a Blessings Journal!** One of the ways you can begin gathering your testimonies is by devoting time each day to write them down. Whether the testimonies are "big" or "small," make a record of what God is doing in your life. You can purchase a notebook to be used exclusively as your "Blessings Journal." You may want to use a simple lined notebook or something a little bit fancier that displays your character and resonates with your personality. Decide what suits you best! The key, though, is not to use this notebook for anything else (like making grocery lists, writing notes for Bible studies, goal-setting, and so forth). This notebook should be treated as a sacred journal that exclusively holds your written testimony.

Your journal will become a very helpful and encouraging resource for you in the future as you look back at what you have written and are able to read about all the wonderful things God has done for you. If you are invited to publicly share your testimony, you will know exactly where to start! So, keep yourself committed to writing in your journal at least once every week. You might pick a particular time of the day or day of the week to record your testimonies.

Feel free to be creative with your writing. You might want to write some testimonies in bullet-point form (just giving the highlights) and others in greater detail. Experience the joy of the Lord and have fun while creating your very own Blessings Journal. Who knows? It could become the basis for a book in the future.

3. **Call a Friend!** Why not take time in prayer to ask God to speak to you about a friend who needs some encouragement? Once the Lord reveals who you should call, ask Him to remind you of a testimony in your life that you could share with them. Then, pick up the phone and call your friend, expecting the Spirit to open a power portal of His goodness as you share your testimony.

# LESSON 9

# ESTABLISHING PLACES OF POWER

Before you begin this lesson, read chapter 9 of *Power Portals*.

*"Open up, O heavens, and pour out your righteousness. Let the earth open wide so salvation and righteousness can sprout up together. I, the Lord, created them."*
—Isaiah 45:8 (NLT)

## HEAVEN IS OPEN FOR US

- Heaven is now open for us because Jesus died for our sins and rose victoriously, ascending into heaven and giving us the gift of the Holy Spirit to reside within us.

- This truth cannot be altered. It is a reality that we can access every day.

- However, we have seen that not every believer is living in an open heaven! What is the proof of this? Many believers themselves are the proof of this because they do not demonstrate the victory Christ won for them. They are living defeated lives.

- An open heaven demands an open earth.

- If we want to experience the blessings of an open heaven, we must be willing to do whatever it takes to connect with the open heavens in order to keep them open over our lives.

- Jesus is our eternal open portal, but we must become His open portals so that His manifest presence is displayed on the earth.

Q: HOW IS BEING AN OPEN PORTAL POSSIBLE? WHAT ARE SOME SPIRITUAL PRINCIPLES FOR HOLDING OPEN THE HEAVENS THAT YOU'VE LEARNED THROUGH THIS STUDY?

- Speaking to His disciples, Jesus said, *"Occupy until I come"* (Luke 19:13).

Q: ARE YOU A PRESENT-DAY DISCIPLE OF CHRIST? WHAT DOES IT LOOK LIKE TO BE HIS DISCIPLE? WHAT IS REQUIRED?

- Jesus also said, *"I will give you the keys (authority) of the kingdom of heaven; and whatever you bind [forbid, declare to be improper and unlawful] on earth will have [already] been bound in heaven, and whatever you loose [permit, declare unlawful] on earth will have [already] been loosed in heaven"* (Matthew 16:19 AMP).
- The keys of the kingdom are used for unlocking heavenly portals on the earth.
- These keys open spiritual doors on earth that correspond with open portals in heaven.

### FIVE KEYS FOR ESTABLISHING AN OPEN PORTAL

#### KEY #1: YOU MUST NOT BE WON OVER BY FAME, FAVOR, OR FINANCE

### READ: PSALM 1:1–3

- This key deals with our true motives.
- Ask yourself the following questions:
  - » Whose attention are you seeking?
  - » What position do you desire?
  - » Are you only in it for the money?
- Your heart must be set to seek the attention of God and God alone.
- Humility before God should always take priority in our lives.
- If we can get our hearts right about money, we can get our hearts right about anything.

#### KEY #2: YOU MUST GIVE YOUR HEART TO PRAYER IN THE SECRET PLACE

### READ: MATTHEW 6:6

- Prayer is another key the Spirit has given us in this hour for maintaining open heavens.

- When Jesus prayed after His baptism, the heavens opened. (See Luke 3:21.)

- Jesus taught us to pray that the heavens would continue to be opened to earth. (See Matthew 6:10.)

- The Spirit desires to bring us into the flow of "praying in the Spirit."

- What God can accomplish through our prayers is absolutely miraculous.

## Q: WHAT HAPPENED IN ACTS 12:1–17 AND IN ACTS 16:22–34? HOW WAS PRAYER CONNECTED TO THESE BREAKTHROUGHS?

- Release comes as we learn how to pray in the flow of the Spirit. This is what brings heaven to earth in our lives.

- When we pray in the Spirit, we can never be wrong because it is God praying through us.

### KEY #3: YOU MUST LOVE THE LORD YOUR GOD WITH ALL YOUR HEART

## READ: MATTHEW 22:37

- We must draw near to God with our hearts and not just with our lips.

- Our heart is the initial meeting point for heaven and earth. Once heaven touches our heart, it will automatically flow out through our lips.

- *"I will give him the key to the house of David—the highest position in the royal court. When he opens doors, no one will be able to close them; when he closes doors, no one will be able to open them"* (Isaiah 22:22 NLT).

- In the Bible, keys represent authority.

- David lived his life as a worshipper of God. The key of David is the authority of praise and worship.

- Revelation 3:7 says that Jesus Christ holds the key of David.

## Q: WHERE IS JESUS CHRIST RIGHT NOW? WHERE IS THE KEY OF DAVID?

- This is a supernatural key that is given to believers along with the authority to open and shut doors in the Spirit realm through praise and worship.

- God inhabits (is enthroned upon) the praises of His people. (See Psalm 22:3 KJV.)

- The heavenly Father is seeking those who will worship Him in Spirit and in truth. (See John 4:23–24.)

## Q: WHAT DO THE ABOVE SCRIPTURE PASSAGES MEAN TO YOU?

- If there has been a blockage or resistance in the realm of the first or second heaven, when we let the high praises of God come forth from our innermost being, the light within is released, and God draws near, so that nothing can impede us.

### KEY #4: YOUR MOTIVES MUST BE PURE AND NOT ABOUT SELFISH GAIN

### READ: MATTHEW 5:8

- In the place of worship, it is important to examine your heart and your motives.

- God will reveal things to us in worship that have not been revealed to us previously.

## Q: WHY DO YOU WANT TO BE KNOWN AS A POWER PORTAL? IS IT FOR SELF-RECOGNITION, OR IS IT FOR THE GLORY OF GOD?

- We must desire to be seen only so that Christ can be seen in us.

- The more we open ourselves to God, the more "heart checks" we will experience.

- Who is in control of your life? We must learn how to let God fight our battles for us.

## Q: WHAT DOES IT MEAN TO ALLOW GOD TO FIGHT OUR BATTLES? HOW WILL YOU DO THIS IN PRACTICAL WAYS?

- In the glory realm, there is no warfare. In the glory, we are positioned in a place of rest. In the glory, we're learning to trust God to a greater degree.

- Open up and let the river flow!

- When the river of God comes in, the spirit of heaviness is broken, and you can take off your garments of mourning and put on your garments of praise. (See Isaiah 61:3.)

### KEY #5: YOU MUST HAVE A PASSION FOR THE THINGS OF GOD

- *"Passion for your house has consumed me"* (Psalm 69:9 NLT).

- A passion for Jesus changes everything!

- Heavenly passion is divine energy.

- A person with a passionate heart for the things of God is unstoppable!

- When we begin to do on earth what is done in heaven, then heaven responds and changes our earthly reality.

- Heaven is the model, the blueprint, the pattern.

- As we bring heaven to earth, everything about our world will begin to change.

## REVIEW QUESTIONS

(Page numbers correspond to the *Power Portals* book.)

1. "_____ up, O heavens, and pour out your righteousness. Let the earth _____ wide so salvation and righteousness can _____ _____ together. I, the LORD, created them" (Isaiah 45:8 NLT). (p. 189)

2. Not every believer is living in an _____ heaven! An open _____ demands an open _____. (p. 189)

3. Write out Matthew 16:19 in *The Amplified Version*: (p. 190)

   _____

   _____

   _____

   _____

   _____

   _____

4. Name the five keys the Spirit gave us for opening effective portals on the earth: (pp. 193–194, 198, 203, 205)

   1. _____

   2. _____

   3. _____

   4. _____

   5. _____

5. What is meant by the phrase "the key of David"? (p. 199)

   _____

   _____

   _____

   _____

   _____

   _____

6. Give a biblical example of a "sound portal," and then give an example of how this revelation can be applied to your own life. (pp. 200–201)

_____

_____

_____

_____

_____

_____

7. In an open heaven, as God's people praise His name, and His manifest presence is suddenly felt, everyone can _____ in the Spirit and _____ from heaven. (p. 204)

## ACTIVATIONS

1. **Take the Five-Keys Assessment.** For this personal activation, I want to encourage you to rate yourself on the "Five Keys for Establishing an Open Portal" described in this lesson and on pages 193–206 of *Power Portals*. The number 1 represents the lowest score (indicating need for improvement), and the number 10 represents the highest score (indicating victory). Circle the number that you feel best describes your current condition. This is a self-assessment, and it is important to be honest with yourself. In this way, you will be able to identify the areas in your life where you are succeeding and other areas where you may need improvement.

Key #1: You must not be won over by fame, favor, or finance.

1   2   3   4   5   6   7   8   9   10

Key #2: You must give your heart to prayer in the secret place.

1   2   3   4   5   6   7   8   9   10

Key #3: You must love the Lord your God with all your heart.

1   2   3   4   5   6   7   8   9   10

Key #4: Your motives must be pure and not about selfish gain.

1   2   3   4   5   6   7   8   9   10

Key #5: You must have a passion for the things of God.

1   2   3   4   5   6   7   8   9   10

Now that you have completed this self-assessment, seek the Lord and ask Him to help you take meaningful steps toward improving any area in which you feel you are lacking. Write down what He speaks to you:

_____

_____

_____

_____

_____

2. **Ask the Spirit for a Prayer-Walking Strategy.** This is a group activation, although an individual can also go on a prayer walk. The main purpose of a prayer walk is to seek God regarding the needs of a region or community. You can trust that the Spirit will reveal to you Satan's hidden agendas for your area and heaven's

solutions to them. Spirit-birthed prayers are powerful and have the ability to shift an atmosphere. Expect the glory of God to show up as you pray, and make room for miracles to happen along the way. I also suggest making sure that your prayer walk is not too long. It's not as much about the amount of distance covered as it is about saturating an area with the manifest presence of God. An hour is usually a good amount of time to spend on an initial prayer walk. Of course, the Spirit may lead you differently, so going with His guidance is always best. Here are three steps you can take to prepare yourself for occupying territory for the Spirit.

**Step 1:**

Find some other glory intercessors who can join you on a prayer walk. Of course, it is okay to do a prayer walk alone, but it is always better to cover a region with corporate prayer. (See Matthew 18:20.) In this way, as a group, you will begin seeing and hearing in the Spirit regarding your region. There is wisdom in the counsel of many. (See Proverbs 15:22; 24:6.) Ask the Holy Spirit to reveal the names of other believers who might go on a pray walk with you. Write the names below:

_____

_____

_____

_____

_____

**Step 2:**

Before beginning a prayer walk, plan a specific route around your region, with stops at significant locations and buildings. Seek the Lord's guidance regarding the specific places where you should go. For example, you may want to pray at the site of a local government building (such as city hall or the state capitol building), a local school, or another place where many people gather. As you seek the Lord, write down the places He reveals to you:

_____

_____

_____

_____

_____

**Step 3:**

Now that you've identified specific places to focus on in your prayer walk, print out a map of your local area so that you can effectively walk this route. On the printed map, mark the exact locations where you will stop, and write down the prayer points that you will cover while you're on-site. You can either list some prayer points below or use a separate sheet of paper that you attach to the map for this purpose:

_____

_____

_____

_____

_____

**Step 4:**

When you go out on your prayer walk, it is important to pray in the Spirit. You can trust that the Holy Spirit will begin to speak to you as you do this. Let Him lead you and guide you (be open to any change in direction He gives you), and allow Him to bring His insight as you pray on-site. Declare the glory of God over your community, activate and release angel armies to move into divine position, and be watchful of favored opportunities and divine connections. Stay on point and remain in prayer. Remember to be respectful of others while you do these things. It is not necessary for your prayers to be loud. Instead, it is important for your prayers to be powerful, and that will happen as you are led by the Spirit of God.

**Step 5:**

Allow time for the members of your prayer team to share what they sense the Spirit is speaking to them. Then, you will be able to address these issues together through prayer and invite God's power to come and manifest His glory. Keep a journal of what God is showing you and document the miraculous transformations that take place as you continue to occupy territory for the Lord.

Now…go and do it! Remember God's promise in Joshua 1:3: *"Every place that the sole of your foot shall tread upon, that have I given to you, as I said to Moses."*

# ANSWER KEY

## LESSON 1: WHAT IS A POWER PORTAL?

1. "a doorway, gate, or other entrance, especially a large and imposing one"

2. doors of transition

3. On the road to Damascus, Paul (still known as Saul) experienced a blinding light that came directly from heaven, shining upon him and knocking him to the ground. In this portal, God's voice spoke to Paul with clarity, giving him specific direction for his life.

4. There is a connection between heaven and earth (verse 12). Angels are actively involved in the lives of God's people (verse 12). God desires that you hear His voice (verse 13). God wants to remind you of your spiritual inheritance (verse 13). A generational blessing is available for you and your descendants (verse 13). Divine protection surrounds you (verse 15).

5. A sudden, awesome realization comes. An abundance of healing manifests. Spontaneous joy erupts. Signs and wonders manifest. Angelic activity intensifies. Spiritual dreams and visions increase. Extravagant provision appears.

6. power portals; heaven

7. purple: royalty; blue: the prophetic realm or prophetic revelation; red: healing; orange: power

## LESSON 2: FINDING YOUR WAY

1. the opening of spiritual portals

2. portal of God's glory

3. door; gateway

4. (Give your own answer.)

5. *"I am the way, the truth, and the life: no man comes to the Father, but by Me."*

6. (1) He is the only portal to God. (2) He is the portal of escape. (3) He is the portal into the holiest. (4) He is the portal into *"a new and living way."* (5) He is the portal of truth. (6) He is the portal into the *"right way."* (7) He is the portal of righteousness.

7. around; upon; within

## LESSON 3: RECOGNIZING CHRIST IN YOU

1.  spheres; atmospheres

2.  new; creation

3.  Their proclamation is driven by what they continually see before them. Their eyes are on the One who sits upon the throne. They constantly behold something new and different about Him that they have never seen before. They see new realms of His beauty, new realms of His majesty, new realms of His wonder, new realms of His miraculous power, new realms of His judgment, new realms of His goodness, and new realms of His mercy and grace. Each time, they are inspired to cry out, "Holy!"

4.  greater; wider

5.  (Give your own answer.)

6.  yourself

7.  glory; vision; dream; divine potential

## LESSON 4: THE HEAVENS ARE OPEN

1.  heavens; earth

2.  (Give your own answer.)

3.  the Temple Mount

4.  faith; spiritual vortexes

5.  place

6.  awakening; connect

7.  Sometimes, God will share with you His mysteries in the secret place, and these mysteries must remain hidden in your heart. They are given to you for your own personal benefit and spiritual development, and it is not necessary (or appropriate) for you to share them or even let others know that you have received them from the Lord. These are intimate moments with God that are meant for you and Him alone.

## LESSON 5: SYNCHRONIZING WITH THE SPIRIT

1.  enmity

2.  small; big

3.  Peter and his business partners had fished all night without catching anything. After Peter obeyed Jesus's word, their nets were full to the breaking point, and they filled two boats with the fish they caught. Peter fell down at Jesus's knees, expressed a sense of his sinfulness, and was astonished.

4.  (Give your own answer.)

5.  overeating; drunkenness

6.  (Give your own answer.)

7.  (1) the heart (spirit); (2) the mouth; (3) the eyes and ears; (4) the mind; (5) the innermost being; (6) the hands; (7) the feet

## LESSON 6: THE SEVEN DIMENSIONS OF DIVINE POWER

1. First dimension: *ischys*; forceful power. (Give your own example.)
2. Second dimension: *kratos*; prevailing power. (Give your own example.)
3. Third dimension: *energeia* and *energeō*; energizing power. (Give your own example.)
4. Fourth dimension: *dynamis*; miraculous power. (Give your own example.)
5. Fifth dimension: *exousia*; authoritative power. (Give your own example.)
6. Sixth dimension: *harpazō*; deliverance power. (Give your own example.)
7. Seventh dimension: *episkiazō*; overshadowing power. (Give your own example.)

## LESSON 7: OPENING PERSONAL PORTALS

1. pride/humility; unforgiveness/forgiveness; anger/self-control; depression/joy; loneliness/connection; fear and anxiety/love; jealousy/thankfulness
2. (Give your own answer.)
3. frankincense, sacred frankincense, lemon, and Melrose
4. (Give your own answer.)
5. belly; innermost being
6. prosperity; prosperity; privilege; flow
7. They are anointed to take territory and walk in God's promises.

## LESSON 8: CREATING SPIRITUAL PATHWAYS

1. "a solemn declaration or affirmation made for the purpose of establishing or proving some fact. An open attestation of profession; a witness of evidence, proof of some truth"
2. (Give your own answer.)
3. stand up in that portal; run into it; lift up your hands to receive what is being dispersed; open your palms in front of you (as though receiving a gift); soak in the presence of that encounter
4. That one of the ways we overcome is by our testimony.
5. (1) a portal of victory; (2) a portal of blessing; (3) a portal of prophetic decree; (4) a portal of creative miracles
6. things that are true, things that are honest, things that are just, things that are pure, things that are lovely, things that are of good report, virtuous, and praiseworthy
7. (Give your own answer.)

## CHAPTER 9: ESTABLISHING PLACES OF POWER

1. open; open; sprout up
2. open; heaven; earth
3. *"I will give you the keys (authority) of the kingdom of heaven; and whatever you bind [forbid, declare to be improper and unlawful] on earth will have [already] been bound in heaven, and whatever you loose [permit, declare lawful] on earth will have [already] been loosed in heaven."*

4. (1) You must not be won over by fame, favor, or finance. (2) You must give your heart to prayer in the secret place. (3) You must love the Lord your God with all your heart. (4) Your motives must be pure and not about selfish gain. (5) You must have a passion for the things of God.

5. This is a supernatural key that is given to believers along with the authority to open and shut doors in the Spirit realm through praise and worship.

6. The Israelites cried out in their slavery (Exodus 3:9–10); trumpet blasts and loud shouts resounded at Jericho's defeat (Joshua 6:5, 20); there was a sound of heavenly hosts marching in the tops of the balsam trees (2 Samuel 5:23–25); David and Isaiah were both instructed to sing a new song (Psalm 40:3 and Isaiah 42:10); God roars against His enemies (Isaiah 42:13); Jesus prayed with loud cries and tears (Hebrews 5:7); the Holy Spirit sounded like a mighty, rushing wind (Acts 2:2); the early church spoke in new tongues (Acts 2:4); all of creation groans (Romans 8:22). (Give your own answer for the second part of this question.)

7. see; hear

# RECOMMENDED RESOURCES

**OTHER BOOKS BY JOSHUA MILLS:**

*31 Days of Health, Wealth & Happiness*

*31 Days to a Breakthrough Prayer Life*

*31 Days to a Miracle Mindset*

*Atmosphere: Creating a Realm for Miracles & Success*

*Encountering Your Angels: Biblical Proof That Angels Are Here to Help*

*The Glory: Scriptures & Prayers to Manifest God's Presence in Your Life*

*Moving in Glory Realms: Exploring Dimensions of Divine Presence**

*Positioned for Prosperity: Unlocking the Realms of Blessing, Favor & Increase*

*Power Portals: Awaken Your Connection to the Spirit Realm**

*Seeing Angels: How to Recognize and Interact with Your Heavenly Messengers**

*Simple Supernatural: Keys to Living in the Glory Realm*

*Third Day Prayers*

*Time & Eternity: Taking Authority Over Your Day!*

**ALBUMS BY JOSHUA MILLS (EITHER CD OR DIGITAL DOWNLOAD):**

*Activating Angels in Your Life* (2-disc CD)

*Experience His Glory*

*Receive Your Healing*

*Reversing the Clock*

*Also available as an audiobook

Joshua Mills's resources are available online at:

www.JoshuaMills.com

# ABOUT THE AUTHOR

Joshua Mills is an internationally recognized, ordained minister of the gospel, as well as a recording artist and keynote conference speaker. He is also the author of more than twenty books and training manuals. His books with Whitaker House include *Power Portals*, *Moving in Glory Realms*, and *Seeing Angels*, all with corresponding study guides, and *Encountering Your Angels*.

Joshua is well known for the supernatural atmosphere that he carries and for his unique insights into the glory realm and prophetic sound. Wherever Joshua ministers, the Word of God is confirmed by miraculous signs and wonders that testify of Jesus Christ. For more than twenty years, he has helped people discover the life-shifting truths of salvation, healing, and deliverance for spirit, soul, and body.

Joshua and his wife, Janet, cofounded International Glory Ministries and have ministered in over seventy-five nations on six continents. Featured together in several film documentaries and print articles, they have ministered to millions around the world through radio, television, and their weekly webcast, *Glory Bible Study*. Their ministry is located in both Palm Springs, California, and London, Ontario, Canada, where they live with their three children, Lincoln, Liberty, and Legacy.

www.joshuamills.com

# Welcome to Our House!

*We Have a Special Gift for You*

It is our privilege and pleasure to share in your love of Christian books. We are committed to bringing you authors and books that feed, challenge, and enrich your faith.

To show our appreciation, we invite you to sign up to receive a specially selected **Reader Appreciation Gift**, with our compliments. Just go to the Web address at the bottom of this page.

God bless you as you seek a deeper walk with Him!

WHITAKER
HOUSE